It's a ... f Fact

In this new book from Routledge and MiddleWeb, author Angie Miller shows how you can turn your students into informed citizens by teaching them how to research effectively. In today's information-saturated world research skills have moved beyond fact-finding, into fact-sifting, fact-sorting, and fact-assessing. Miller shows you how to help students check sources, take good notes, make use of information, and synthesize and present information across the subject areas. She also shows how to make research a daily practice, not a one-time essay or project. With examples and online handouts you can use immediately, this practical book is a valuable resource for educators seeking to engage students in their work and encourage them toward higher level thinking.

Angie Miller is a middle and high school teacher–librarian in New Hampshire. The 2011 New Hampshire Teacher of the Year, the recipient of the 2017 New Hampshire Library Program of the Year, a TED speaker, and a National Geographic Teacher Fellow, she writes, speaks, and runs professional development that advocates for the teaching profession and promotes the empowerment of student voice across the country.

Also Available from
Routledge Eye On Education and MiddleWeb
www.routledge.com/collections/11190

Write, Think, Learn: Tapping the Power of Daily Student Writing Across the Content Areas
Mary K. Tedrow

Creating Citizens: Teaching Civics and Current Events in the History Classroom, 6–9
Sarah Cooper

Close Reading the Media: Literacy Lessons and Activities for Every Month of the School Year
Frank W. Baker

The Genius Hour Guidebook: Fostering Passion, Wonder, and Inquiry in the Classroom
Denise Krebs and Gallit Zvi

STEM by Design: Strategies and Activities for Grades 4–8
Anne Jolly

The Flexible ELA Classroom: Practical Tools for Differentiated Instruction in Grades 4–8
Amber Chandler

History Class Revisited: Tools and Projects to Engage Middle School Students in Social Studies
Jody Passanisi

Two Teachers in the Room: Strategies for Co-Teaching Success
Elizabeth Stein

It's a Matter of Fact

Teaching Students
Research Skills in Today's
Information-Packed World

Angie Miller

Routledge
Taylor & Francis Group

NEW YORK AND LONDON

All About the Middle Grades
MiddleWeb

First published 2018
by Routledge
711 Third Avenue, New York, NY 10017

and by Routledge
2 Park Square, Milton Park, Abingdon, Oxon, OX14 4RN

Routledge is an imprint of the Taylor & Francis Group, an informa business

© 2018 Taylor & Francis

Library of Congress Cataloging-in-Publication Data
A catalog record for this book has been requested

ISBN: 978-1-138-30278-5 (hbk)
ISBN: 978-1-138-30280-8 (pbk)
ISBN: 978-0-203-73168-0 (ebk)

Typeset in Palatino
by Florence Production Ltd, Stoodleigh, Devon, UK

Download the eResources at www.routledge.com/9781138302808

Contents

Meet the Author

Angie Miller is a middle and high school teacher–librarian in New Hampshire. The 2011 New Hampshire Teacher of the Year, the recipient of the 2017 New Hampshire Library Program of the Year, a TED speaker, and a National Geographic Teacher Fellow, she writes, speaks, and runs professional development that advocates for the teaching profession and promotes the empowerment of student voice across the country.

eResources

Keep an eye out for the eResources icon throughout this book, which indicates a resource is available online. Resources mentioned in this book can be downloaded, printed, used to copy/paste text, and/or manipulated to suit your individualized use. You can access these downloads by visiting the book product page on our website: www.routledge.com/9781138302808. Then click on the tab that reads "eResources" and then select the file(s) you need. The file(s) will download directly to your computer.

Come, seek, for search is the foundation of fortune; every success depends upon facing the heart.

Rumi

The world doesn't care what you know. What the world cares about is what you do with what you know.

Tony Wagner

Introduction:
Why Research?

Today's World

We're in the car driving home, and my 14-year-old son and his best friend are in the back seat, engaged in their usual sports banter. "Did you know Jake Peavy is legally blind?" my son asks his friend, Henry. "What?" says Henry. "A pitcher can't be blind! You're making that up."

But my son is insistent. "No," he says. "He is legally blind. I'm not making it up." He pulls out his phone and types "Jake Peavy blind" into the search bar and starts reading an ESPN article aloud. Henry laughs and asks, "What the heck does that even mean? I mean, can you be *illegally* blind?" Another quick search and they are both hovering over the device, reading the definition of "legally blind."

These two boys, along with most every other kid across the country, are growing up with search engines in their back pockets, integrating research into their day-to-day conversations, proving their points and investigating where they are more curious. But this is not just a generational thing—we are all living this lifestyle. With all-the-time digital access to news, sports, weather, and entertainment, we have evolved, seemingly overnight, into a research culture, where answers to our questions are literally at our fingertips. Daily conversations with family, friends, and colleagues often result in looking up information or pulling up previously read articles as reference. Even our youngest students know they can look information up when they need or want it. While our plugged-in habits come with a certain level of concern, they also make our reality extremely exciting: we are standing in the moment when research has become a way of life.

The research nerd in me loves this! But like most things wonderful, our research-drenched culture does come with some grave, possible dangers. If we do not assess the information we read for credibility, question an author's motive, or make meaning of what we read, we are at risk of breeding ignorance in an uninformed populace. This gift of research at our fingertips could be instrumental in the progression of creative, innovative thinking, catapulting us into a future of critical thinking, or it could be our greatest downfall, plunging us into a realm of irresponsibility.

Researching well may be the most important academic skill we can help nurture in our students.

How Exactly Does Research Help Our Students?

Research builds important inquiry strategies for college and workplace success.

Anyone reading this book likely believes our students need to walk away from high school with a toolkit of good research skills that they can readily use in college and the workplace, where research is an ongoing expectation. In college, students are asked to research at all levels of their education in all disciplines, using higher-order thinking skills. In the workforce, employers want employees who can ask good questions, dig in and assess resources, and draw conclusions to create new, innovative ideas. Moving from high school to college or the workplace doesn't have to be an overwhelming leap for our students if we give them the right kinds of research tools in middle and high school.

Our standards agree. The Common Core State Standards (CCSS) emphasize that research is so important it should be embedded throughout every discipline, reminding us that research is a personalized, ongoing lifestyle, not just an educational experience. They state:

> To be ready for college, workforce training, and life in a technological society, students need the ability to gather, comprehend, evaluate, synthesize, and report on information and ideas, to conduct original research in order to answer questions or solve problems, and to analyze and create a high volume and extensive range of print and nonprint texts in media forms old and new. The need to conduct research and to produce and consume media is embedded into every

aspect of today's curriculum. In like fashion, research and media skills and understandings are embedded throughout the Standards rather than treated in a separate section

(Common Core Standards, www.corestandards.org/
ELA-Literacy/introduction/key-design-consideration/)

Within the CCSS, teachers will find standards that point to short- and long-term research projects in all areas of study, focusing on reading, assessing, analyzing, and synthesizing material, piggybacking on the previously published positions of all national major literary professional organizations.

The Next Generation Science Standards, the C3 Framework for Social Studies Standards, and the American Association of School Library's 21st Century Standards also delineate the importance of research integration in our curricula as well. The professional organizations that we rely on for guidance in our careers agree: research is one of the most important skills we can help our students develop in life and school.

The Bloomberg Job Recruiter Report—a survey that takes into account the feedback of 600 companies and 1,320 job recruiters—notes that the skills most desired, but hardest to find, include creative problem solving, strategic thinking, and excellent communication skills (Bloomberg 2015). These three skills are all part of the research process. When students know how to inquire and support their assertions with facts, they become synthesizers who can pull together multiple resources to solve problems. They have to think strategically to draw conclusions. And they must be able to communicate their ideas clearly in order to relay their research findings. By strengthening these skills in students, we are indeed preparing them for working in the real world.

Yet, too often, our conversations with students about how to research haven't really shifted much over the years, while the landscapes of resources around them have. This has culminated in a mismatch of performance and expectation. We often over-assume what our "digital natives" know and proceed even if they don't. A study of college freshmen showed that, "the Google-centric search skills that [college] freshmen bring from high school only get them so far with finding and using trusted sources they need for fulfilling college research assignments" (Head 2013, p. 1). In fact, most college freshmen report that their high schools did not prepare them for college-level research (Head 2013).

There is imminent need for our students to research well in their futures, and if we start breathing fire into their passions and interest early, we can ensure their preparedness for both school and the job market.

Research helps students make meaning of their world.

When research plays an integral role in our students' lives, they can explain why we do things and argue how we can be better. They can narrate how we came to be, where we should go, and why we are the way we are. Research helps our students understand science and humanity, while developing the empathy and understanding that is necessary for finding sustainable solutions. It helps them contribute to important conversations in knowledgeable ways that move their communities forward. Good research helps them speak passionately from the heart in smart ways, using their heads. It recognizes that it is not enough to know, they must also think and act.

Research allows our students to understand themselves. In my library, I have students come in and ask for nonfiction books on religion, alcoholism, drug abuse, mental illness, depression, death, the military, eating disorders. Our students wrestle with issues larger than the small world we've built for them, and while they need fiction books that have characters who look and act like them, they crave nonfiction resources that helps them grasp the terms by which they live.

They are trying to make sense of their world, their families, and themselves. By arming them with research skills, we can aid them in this mission.

Research Skills Are an Act of Citizenship

Are we teaching the kinds of inquiry skills our students require to successfully navigate this world they live in? Scroll through the comment section of any online news story, and you will discover the pitfalls of bad research practices. In fact, school aside, if there's any singular thing I ever want for my students, it is not to be the person writing vitriolic, poorly researched falsities at the bottom of a piece of journalism. Research to support opinion, research to drive missions, research to guide important democratic decisions—these are essential acts of citizenship in today's media-drenched lifestyle. My agenda-of-the-heart is that we can help launch responsible and ethical researchers through deliberate guidance in all of our classrooms.

During the 2016 presidential election, one that will always be remembered for its polarized arguments, a group of researchers read and categorized every Facebook-posted article for one week on three right-wing media sites, three left-wing media sites, and three mainstream media sites. They discovered that 38% of the right-wing articles were false, 19% of the left-wing articles were false, and 0% of the mainstream site articles were false. The more alarming part of the study came in the consumption of these articles. The more false an article was, the more it was liked and shared, and when people liked or shared articles, the algorithms of Facebook fed them more of the same, resulting in a large percentage of our population believing false information to make a decision about who should be the president of the United States of America (Silverman 2016).

As our citizenship relies more and more on social media for information and we watch echo chambers confirm biases, we need to ensure that our students have the research skills to assess the credibility of what they read.

I cannot emphasize enough: well-developed research skills are important for the future of our country and integral for any democratic society to thrive.

But, How?

It is easy to assume that our "digitally native" kids like Elliot and Henry know how to research well because they have grown up with research tools and an abundance of information available to them at all times. But more information and tools does not correlate with better skills. Students still require guidance to master the complex, high-level skills that research requires. To do this successfully, there are several things to keep in mind.

Research as a Creative Act

Gone are the days of regurgitation. Anybody can look up facts, and anybody can report those facts back. Yet, too often, in middle and high school research, we are asking students to fact find and not research. There's a difference—fact-finding is a matter of looking up and repeating facts readily available to anybody. Research is a matter of making meaning from those facts. It's a matter of crafting intelligent responses and new ideas from facts. It's a matter of creating knowledge. When we teach students how to research, we must provide opportunities for them to make meaning of the information they find (see Chapter 2). Synthesizing multiple sources to draw original conclusions engages our students in their work and encourages them to move to higher level thinking.

We have all heard how we are preparing our students for jobs that have not been created yet. And employers want workers who are innovative and creative. Dean Kamen boldly declares that, "success is measured by the rate of innovation . . . [it] drives us to the next level" (Kamen in Wagner 2012). Research has the potential to ignite curiosity and innovation. When students use their research to create meaning, support arguments, and develop solutions, we are showing them how to take risks with their learning. And those who are willing to take risks are more likely to innovate.

When we implement research into our curricula, we should be implementing creativity as well, showing students ways to create meaning, to support arguments, or to develop solutions. No more regurgitating facts that are already common knowledge.

My daughter, who works at her university library, teaches college freshmen how to use the library for their research projects. When I texted her one afternoon and asked what she wished my high school seniors knew about research she exclaimed, "That research is FUN!!! :) So many kids think research is boring—but it's so fun because you can learn whatever you want!" Research assignments need to inspire original thinking, purpose, and motivation with final products that inspire the audience and the creator. The process should spark students' curiosity and never dull their learning, encouraging them to create, not regurgitate.

First and foremost, research should always be an act of creation.

Research as an Explicitly Taught Task in Every Discipline

I was working with a group of high school social studies teachers one day, looking at where and how they teach research in their department. Each declared that the teacher before them had already taught the students how to research, so they didn't need to. Once they looked around the table and heard this collective admission, one of them said, "Oh boy. If none of us actually teach kids how to conduct research, we could send them off to college with 8th grade research skills!"

Yes. Exactly. There is great danger in assuming that somebody else has taught the skills you want students to use. There is even greater danger in assuming that what you want to happen in science or history class was taught in the English room.

In the ideal world, schools will develop a research continuum that addresses all grade levels and departments and ensures a research progression that becomes more sophisticated with each year (see Chapter 8). When that can't or doesn't happen, we have to individually assess what our students know and which skills we need to introduce or revisit.

Have you ever heard of The Curse of Knowledge? It's a term used to describe how we often expect others to know what we know. A friend of mine doesn't wash her fine hair every day when she takes a shower. One day, her 12-year-old, stinky stepson came home from practice and she told him he needed to go take a shower. When he came out of the bathroom 15 minutes later, his hair was dry. "Did you take a shower?" she asked. Yes, he had. "But your hair isn't wet," she said. He stared at her before saying, "You told me to take a shower, not to wash my hair." You see, my friend naturally assumed that "Go take a shower" included the process of washing his hair, but he thought that it was two separate processes. Her curse of knowledge (showers = washing hair) created assumptions about how explicit she needed to be in her directions.

Telling students to "research" or to "take notes" or to "write a thesis statement" without spending some time talking about how-tos and modeling strategies, banks on what we know how to do, and what we think our students already know. The *Harvard Business Review* calls this a "vague strategy statement" (Heath 2006) that is a byproduct of the Curse of Knowledge. Too often, we think that students understand directions because in our minds they make sense. But in fact, without explicit instruction, they have to come to their own definitions of the terminology. When we offer abstract strategies to our students without the tangible steps to meet those goals, they adopt harmful practices.

One year I was working with a group of students whose history project notes were all in quotation marks. When the teacher and I met with them to discuss plagiarism, they were upset. "Last year our teacher told us to put it into our own words and if we couldn't, to put quotes around it." Without any strategies to put their findings into their own words, they had, collectively, begun to just rely on quoting nearly every passage from their resources.

Explicitness in our practice will help avoid the ambiguity that can come from our assumptions.

Research as a Habit

Not every research undertaking has to be a grand endeavor with a polished, culminating project. While these are necessary at times, every assignment doesn't have to be a full-fledged one that covers every little step! Some projects can simply focus on assessing resources, while others may add note-taking and organizing information to them.

When embarking on projects, I watch students want to skip the smaller steps of research—assessing and keeping track of resources, note-taking, and organizing information to get to the final product. They will open up a slide presentation and start to dump plagiarized facts into it before they even know what their thesis is. I've watched students write entire paragraphs after only researching for 20 minutes. Eager to finish and unsure of how to progress, they skip the important baby steps that we know ensure success.

Mini projects that result in conversation (see Chapter 8 for ideas) instead of a final product can reinforce the earlier, smaller steps of research that students so often skip over as they lay eyes on final products. By interspersing our units with small splashes of research skills, we are reinforcing the harder skills, and our larger, more in-depth units can move at a quicker pace and will bolster student confidence and achievement. Small, frequent opportunities help with mastery of minute skills, developing research habits for our students.

As You Make Your Way through this Book . . .

Teaching research well is teaching thinking. Teaching research well is also hard, and this book will never make an attempt to convince you otherwise. I also know that for many content teachers who have never had any classes or instruction on how to integrate research into their classrooms, the process is daunting. I have two teaching certifications in English and Library Sciences and have never been taught how to integrate research into my curriculum. I understand and honor the overwhelming nature of this task.

Telling students to "go research" is the same as telling us to "teach research." With those simple instructions and no explicit understanding of processes, we can overwhelm ourselves and lose focus on our content. Researching is a forest made up of many smaller trees. Teaching research is the same—it is the collection of minute, deliberate practices that build up to a larger skill. Here is a quick breakdown of skills that both—our students and we—need to successfully master research in the classroom. The rest of this book will be focused on delving deeper into all of these topics.

STUDENT SKILLS NEEDED TO SUCCESSFULLY RESEARCH	
Manage time	Plan, chunk, and work efficiently
Presearch and brainstorm	Search for possible topics that interest them
Use resources	Access and assess credible, timely, relevant sources
Question	Narrow a focus, ask essential and supporting questions
Take notes	Read carefully, paraphrase, summarize, cite, find relevant information, and keep track of resources to avoid plagiarism
Organize materials	Keep track of information for bibliographical purposes
Write a thesis	Make a claim based on their findings and be prepared to support it with research
Organize notes and thoughts	Develop outlines and lists with reflections
Create a final product	Successfully synthesize all material to produce a high-quality, thorough, meaningful product that draws conclusions

SKILLS TEACHERS NEED TO SUPPORT STUDENT LEARNING THROUGH RESEARCH	
Planning backwards	• Where do you want students to be in the end? • Is this realistic in the amount of time you have? • What are your objectives—both research and curriculum? • What are the steps that must be taken?
Thinking conceptually	• What major concepts do you want students to understand? • What background knowledge will they need to be successful? Do they have this or will they need to find more?
Managing kids and time	• How will you keep track of what each student is working on? • How will you help students manage their time? • How much time do you have to conference with each kid during the course of the project?
Helping kids find resources	• What is in your library? • What websites are you willing to accept? • Are there enough resources available at the right reading level for what you are expecting your students to do?
Providing feedback	• How will you give feedback—through writing, face to face, or voice recording?
Assessing	• What are the important concepts and skills that need to be assessed with this project?

Never a fan of prescriptive teaching or formulaic learning, I want to make sure that this book never comes off as a list of "thou shalts." Teaching and learning are equal parts of our personal identity, and how we approach our students, our content, and our classrooms will differ. As acknowledgement of personalizing our teaching instruction alongside our students' experiences, I have reached out to a group of amazing educators from around the country who have contributed their own lesson plans and ideas. While reading these "Taking a Closer Look" sections, sprinkled throughout the book, you will see thematic similarities as well as adaptations to the research process across a variety of grades and subjects. I hope these spark an inner dialogue that allows you to explore and create exciting practices.

In recognition that we are all busy, I have included some time-savers at the end of each chapter: a #tldnr box (for those who aren't savvy with social media language, this stand for "Too Long; Did Not Read") that includes some quotes from the chapter, addressing salient points. And in recognition that changing our practice is hard, I have included a #tryonething box that gives you a gentle nudge to incorporate one small change into your research instruction.

This is not a book for teachers looking for a new way to tackle their once-a-year research project. Rather, it is a resource for 7–12 educators to regularly integrate research skills throughout their curriculum. It is recognition that research today doesn't look the same as it used to. It's encouragement to spark the interest and involvement of our students. It is an attempt to make the difficult nature of teaching research more attainable by offering explanations and processes. It's hope that together we can help guide a generation into deliberate inquiry practices.

After 15 years as an English teacher and a school librarian, I have listened to my students and watched them navigate ever-changing informational landscapes. While research was once about fact-finding, it is now about fact-sifting, fact-sorting, and fact-assessing, but even more importantly, it is about what we do with our facts. Do we use facts responsibly? Do we use facts to support our beliefs? Do we seek factual truth and draw conclusions on what is real? This is where the title of this book is derived. How we use our facts determines the direction of our collective future. Whether or not we use facts to drive our decisions determines the relevance of democracy and tolerance. Research today is a matter of facts.

We live in a technology-driven culture where we can access any sort of news (or fraudulent) story, at any time, and I am more certain with every passing year that helping them become skilled researchers must be one of our greatest priorities. In a society that is so text-driven and data-heavy, we would be remiss to neglect this. Research is the sweet spot where life intersects with education. In order to succeed in school, work, and life, our students need to be able to access and assess, read for nuanced meanings, organize materials from multiple sources, analyze and synthesize data, and write cohesively. And they do not have weeks to do this. Sometimes they need to use all of those skills on the spot. Let's help them.

1

What Are We Asking Students to Do?

Redesigning Assignments to Encourage Creative and Critical Thinking

Drew

I was sitting in a circle with a group of 25 ninth graders, ready to assist them with the annual freshman research project where each student is assigned an important figure from the Renaissance to research. "So, your teachers have given you this huge research project," I said. "Tell me. When you get an assignment like this, what is the hardest part for you?" One notably quick-witted boy, Drew, looked at me with a sarcastic, raised eyebrow, and said out of the side of his mouth, "Caring." The other kids snickered. I refocused them, talking about finding sources and note-taking, but Drew's answer sat stubbornly in the back of my mind.

When I had a moment to sit privately with Drew, I asked him to explain his answer. "What would make you care?" I inquired. He looked at me, that one eyebrow still arched, a tuft of hair over the other eye, and told me that he didn't need my assistance. He would do whatever minimal work he needed to do to get a B and just go on not caring. "But," I interrupted. "What *would* make you care? What *could* get you hypothetically excited about this assignment?"

"I would care about this project if it actually had something to do with me," he told me. "I mean, here I am, researching and spitting out facts about

Donatello—and guess what? I don't care about Donatello. He has nothing to do with me or anything I'm interested in."

"Is there anybody you *would* care about?" I asked him.

"Yeah," he said. And that's when I first got a glimpse into Drew's world. "There's this dude in *Assassin's Creed Renaissance*—his name is Ezio Auditore da Firenze—and he's kind of cool. I want to know if he was real or not."

I encouraged Drew to do a little bit of reading on Ezio, and he discovered that while the character is loosely based on a real historical figure, there is very little documentation to support this, so Ezio's main characteristics are pulled from several historical figures. There was not enough available information. Drew looked at me. "Well, I guess I'll just go back to researching Donatello then," he said, shoulders slumping, resigned.

"Hold on," I stopped him. "What else interests you about this?" He looked at me hesitantly. "Really?" he asked. I nodded. "I want to know what kind of research the people who created *Assassin's Creed* had to do in order to develop this game. I mean, did they actually go to these places? Are the streets the same? Those clothes they wear—is that what people wore? Do they hire historians and stuff?"

This conversation launched a deeper discussion between Drew, the English teacher, and me, and instead of doing a biographical project, Drew worked with us to re-create his assignment, which now was: How would the video game *Assassin's Creed Renaissance* be different if it had actually taken place during the Renaissance?

As Drew jumped into his research over the next few weeks, his arched eyebrow began to relax into the furrows of invested study. He began to tell me how the developers of *Assassin's Creed* form internationally and ethnically diverse groups so as not to have any unintended bias. They visit the cities they create in their video games. They research the history of the time period thoroughly, using primary documents. We watched Drew become more engaged as he learned more about the Renaissance than almost any other kid in the class. Ultimately, he concluded: No, *Assassin's Creed Renaissance* would not be any different—the creators of the game had done such thorough research themselves they were able to stay true to the historical context of the time period, and then he was able to support those findings with specific examples.

Drew's original disconnect is not an anomaly—it is the story of many of our students—and he left me asking myself *What are we asking our students to do?*

What *Are* We Asking Kids to Do? Making the Shift

We've all collected research projects that have been less than inspiring. A list of facts glued onto a poster board. PowerPoint presentations with ten bullets on a page that are all but plagiarized. Essays that are five paragraphs of formulaic writing that, at their best, are boring and at their worst, chaotic and disorganized. Let's agree that this is not the kind of research that encourages critical thinking or creativity.

Too often, when students (and let's be honest, teachers) hear the word "research" they associate it with the tedious, boring process of gathering and reporting on collected facts. And, indeed, the base of all research is fact-finding. But fact-finding is no longer enough in the data-rich society we live in. Instead, we want assignments where students *do something* with their facts. I don't mean put them in a brochure or on a website—no matter how beautiful you make it, regurgitating information is still regurgitating information. What I mean is research should always build to something greater in either an organized classroom conversation, writing, or presenting (see more detailed ideas in Chapter 8). Students need to make meaning of their facts—they need to draw conclusions, argue points, prove ideas, and produce solutions. They don't need to know a list of facts they can look up anytime; they need to understand how their facts work together. And this should be challenging and fun! It should be the inroad to our curriculum where students can freely explore.

If we want research to engage our students and jumpstart creative and critical thinking, we have to intentionally shift our assignments. So how do we shift from these kinds of assignments to those that engage students? First, let's ask some questions while we unpack Drew's case for clues as to why he moved from being an uninterested learner to an enthusiastic one.

Do Our Assignments Offer Choice and Autonomy?

Drew had choice in his final topic, and this gave him autonomy over his work. When students have a voice in which direction they will explore, they will pick subjects that interest them, which will encourage them to work through the harder parts of research. Research is a naturally recursive and sometimes frustrating process, meaning it's normal to have to backtrack and change gears. When students feel ownership of their course, these changes in direction feel more natural to the process and less like they aren't "doing it right." It also makes research something they do rather than something that is being done to them.

Choice doesn't mean providing students with a list of topics to draw from though. While technically, yes, this is still a "choice," this strategy just gives students teacher-directed topics to choose from, not student-driven avenues of learning. Shifting the locus of control from the teacher to the student doesn't mean we throw out all the content or lower the bar; we just change the course so that we guide students through a space that grants them room to investigate larger themes.

Taking the lessons we learned from Drew, the teacher and I readjusted the assignment the following year. Instead of providing a list of famous people from the era, we provided stacks of books, a resource guide of online sources, and our databases, and then asked students to spend a day in the library reading everything they could and choosing something about the Renaissance that they wanted to dig into. From there, they began to develop a focus and eventually their own essential question. Students developed projects like, "What would air travel look like today if da Vinci's airplane model was built during the Renaissance?" and "How did Renaissance fashion influence later fashion movements?" and "How has modern medicine evolved from Renaissance practices?" In all of these studies, students had to look up facts, most certainly, but their ultimate conclusions were drawn by them. They created meaning through their discovery.

Providing choice does not mean asking students to lone-wolf it through curriculum. It is just shifting the locus of control, making the teacher a guide and a resource through the process. Every day that students were in the library working, I checked in on Drew. He always sat away from his friends with his laptop open and notes strewn around him on the table, working independently. He always had something new to talk about with me. Drew had autonomy over his research project and from where I stood, that looked good.

Is There Greater Purpose and Relevancy to Our Assignments?

Stop and think about yourself as a learner for a moment. I'm certain I am not the only teacher who has sat in a stuffy gym for district-provided PD listening to somebody talk about a topic that doesn't feel applicable to me, wanting to get back into my classroom to dig into the work I know is important, wondering *what is the purpose? How is this relevant to my practice?* The documentation I've produced after such sessions has been forgettable, dryly written work that I stuck somewhere in a folder. In contrast, I have spent countless hours researching for this book, building websites for initiatives, and reading and writing about educational issues that matter to me. I have produced work that I am proud of and that I continue to reflect upon.

Purpose drives the paths we take.

And purpose looks different for every person. Sometimes it is about making ourselves a better person. Sometimes it's about sating curiosity. Sometimes it's to serve others. Often it is about proving a point. It always results in intentional learning.

When Drew undertook his new Renaissance project, he had two purposes:

1. He was genuinely curious about the construction of the video game he plays and is considering going into the video game business as a career. He wanted to know what that career path might entail.
2. He belongs to a group of friends and a virtual community who all play *Assassin's Creed*, and he was excited to share this information with them and appreciate the game at a whole new level.

We learned from Drew that purpose is important, and so we started asking students why they were delving into this study and who would be reading it. The following year, a community production of *Romeo and Juliet* was coming to our school, and the students produced an entryway research display that provided context for the play. When learners know that there is a purpose for their work, they connect their learning to their world in relevant ways, and produce higher-quality work.

Relevancy in learning is the magical congruence of what a student *wants* to know and what a student *needs* to know, and that can be a challenging, formidable balance for us to juggle.

This is where research steps in. It is the doorway that connects studies to student interest. Relevancy is intimate and personal. We are passionate about different topics because our collective experiences differ from one another's. *Assassin's Creed* was relevant to Drew's life. If a teacher assigned me an *Assassin's Creed* research project, I would become your worst student: I'd be passive aggressive, roll my eyes, wait until the last minute, and then turn in lukewarm work that bored you. It would not interest me.

We discovered from Drew that it was important to learn about our students as they learned about their topics in order to guide them through the making sense of it. In the Renaissance project, a student who struggled with drug abuse was interested in the role apothecaries played in addiction. Another who had lost her mother to cancer wanted to investigate how illness was treated during the time period. When students are given the skills to connect our content to their worlds, their work will become important to them.

The other day Ian, a 17-year-old boy, asked me if he could tell me about his science research project. He was studying the ecology of *Pokemon Go*—he wanted to see if there were any patterns as to the kinds of ecosystems where different Pokemons could be found across the country. He was looking at adaptations and density of populations. His eyes lit up as he talked to me for 15 minutes about the guide he is hoping to publish to help all *Pokemon Go* players determine where they should travel to successfully capture all of their Pokemons. Halfway through the conversation I had to stop my eyes from glazing over—it is insufficient to say that *Pokemon Go* is not part of anything I care about. But as I listened to the passion in his voice, I had to admire how much he had learned and how he was applying it to his world.

Drew and Ian remind me that if we give learning context and a raison d'être, students will respond. If we make purpose and relevancy the heart of our assignments, we have found the sweet spot in learning.

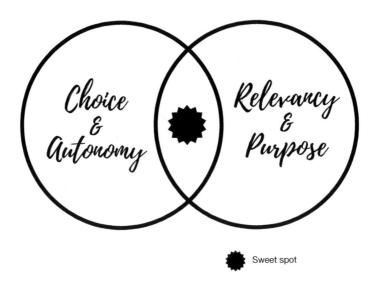

Sweet spot

Figure 1.1 The sweet spot of learning

Making the Shift

I approached two students who had their laptops out and were Googling information for a task I had asked them to do. "Oh, you don't need your laptops for this," I reminded them. "We're not looking information up yet. You're just coming up with a list of questions you have to guide your searches later."

One of the boys looked at me over the top of his glasses. "Yeah," he replied, "but I can just Google a list of questions." I sighed that deeply hidden, internal teacher sigh before saying, "You could . . . but this is about thinking. I want you to think about what you need and want to know for this project."

He continued to look up at me, his face, expressionless. "You want us to *think*?" he asked. "Yes," I responded. "Think." I waited for his sharp response. "Well," he said. "It's about time somebody wants me to think."

"I'm pretty sure every teacher wants you to think," I told him.

"Oh, I'm pretty sure every teacher just wants me to *know stuff*," he retorted. Oof. That hit me hard.

I tell that story hesitantly—because I do believe that we all want our students to think. But after feeling kicked in the stomach, I let that comment settle into the uncomfortable places, reflecting on everything that sat behind it. And it made me re-examine my practices. Do I want kids to *think* or to *know stuff*? After that conversation, I began to frame every research assignment with that tough question, and I was surprised at how it began to shift my assignments. Yes, I want my students to know "stuff," but really I want them to think about that stuff. With thinking, comes knowing.

Shifting to research assignments that uphold these components is tricky, and comes with some doubt and worry. What if they don't find the information we want? What if the available resources are too difficult to read? What if more than one student wants to study the same topic? What if we disagree with their findings? How much time will it take out of our curriculum? How do we control a room of 23 kids all learning at different rates? These fears are real, but they do not present insurmountable obstacles.

We want research to be an autonomous act that ignites curiosity. So first, let's shift our thinking. Instead of asking what do we want our students to *know*, let's ask ourselves, *what do we want them to **understand**?* Students have to know the material to make meaning of it, so if your end goal is understanding, the knowledge will come with that. Conceptual thinking will be inherently driven by concrete knowledge.

What *we* need to understand though as we examine and shift our assignments, is that by asking students to find answers to questions about prescribed topics we have already determined the right answers to, we are not teaching actual research, we are reinforcing hunt and peck skills.

Navigating Levels of Research

Personal research is often used interchangeably for "looking stuff up." But academic research is different, and we need to remind students of that in our language and approach. When it comes to designing academic research assignments for our students, we want to ensure that we are offering opportunities to think critically. In order to do this, we need to consider the different levels of research and how to push beyond the "looking stuff up."

In very basic, teacher-driven research assignments, the topic and questions are provided and there is a right or wrong "right there" answer. An example of this would be asking students how many deaths occur per year because of texting and driving, how it is being handled, what laws are in place, and what penalties are put into action for those who break the laws. Students have to read sources and find the answers to these questions. Usually, students just Google the question and copy and paste the answer.

A principal once said to me, "If a kid can Google the answer, whatever you're teaching needs to be changed." He was right. Is it important for kids to know about texting and driving? Absolutely. Through their research should they collect facts about numbers and deaths? Of course! But do I want them to *know* those numbers or do I want them to *understand* the overarching societal dangers of texting and driving? Academic research is always a matter of what they do with their facts.

If we move the assignment to the next level, we begin to ask students to draw their own conclusions. If we were to tweak the texting and driving assignment, we might instead ask, "What should be done about texting and driving? Use data to support your reasoning." This level of research requires more thinking, as the final answer isn't one that can be typed into a search engine. Students will still need to know the data, but this time they are applying it to a question that is not right or wrong; it is based on their own findings.

And finally, we can move to an even deeper level by guiding students to choose a topic within the broader context of public safety to come up with their own research question (we'll talk about questions later in Chapter 3) and construct a thesis statement that answers that question (Chapter 6). Students may come up with questions like, "If we implemented the same laws as DUI for texting-while-driving, would our accident fatalities drop?" or "How do different states handle texting and what can we learn from that?" In these kinds of assignments, students are given the full reign of choice and autonomy in selecting a relevant topic.

Research projects that focus solely on collecting data, but not using it, simply reinforce hunt and peck research skills and do not require any higher-level thinking. These are okay for quick activities that begin a new unit to build base knowledge or to jumpstart whole group conversations, but let's not confuse fact-finding with research. By middle school we should be moving students to assignments that solely encourage drawing independent conclusions, and by high school, our students should be undertaking entirely student-driven research assignments as much as possible.

SHIFTING OUR ASSIGNMENTS

Instead of . . .	. . . try . . .	. . . and then move to . . .
How do antibiotics work?	Are we overusing antibiotics? Explore the benefits and dangers of our usage.	Explore a bio-ethical issue that concerns you, offering possible solutions.
Give a report on a country. Include population, size, government, education system, famous sites, and holidays.	Pretend you are a travel agent selling a trip to a country. What would your audience need to know? Why should they go there?	Explore a major issue that a country of your choice is currently dealing with and offer a solution.
Write a biography about a famous person. Include their childhood background, education, life struggles, and what they have done.	How did the person you are researching make an impact on today's world?	Choose a person you are curious about and make a connection to an issue today.
Research weaponry from the Civil War. Include major weapons used, how and when they were invented, how they were used, and what their impact on the war was.	What role did weaponry in the Civil War play?	Choose a contributing factor to the Civil War's outcome and explore its impact.
Research a mental illness. Include information about the number of people afflicted, symptoms, and treatment.	Are we doing enough to address mental illness?	Explore a mental illness that you are interested in, making connections to the greater world.

When designing (or re-designing) new units, contemplating what the most important concepts that we want our students to understand is key. All of the smaller facts that we are hoping they know will be attained as they move towards higher-level thinking and more complex research. When looking at the shift, from teacher-driven to student-driven, you will notice that the scope changes and the language becomes more open. Often, we are so concerned that our students won't find the right answers, that we provide them with so much structure they can't go wrong . . . or learn. We are fearful of the vague, because we have things to do and content to cover. But in doing that, we sometimes provide so much structure in our assignments, that we ultimately do the thinking for our students.

Making an intentional plan to shift our assignments from teacher-driven to student-driven doesn't have to be a painstaking process. It just requires a little reflection. Using a chart like this one can help shift our assignments as we start to make our plans.

INITIAL RESEARCH PLANNING SHEET	
What major concepts do I want students to understand?	Natural disasters have lasting impacts on a society.
Is there flexibility in the topic?	Yes—students can choose an event and a location.
Does this assignment encourage independently drawn conclusions?	Yes—students will conclude how the chosen locale has handled the repercussions. There is no right or wrong; they will all be conclusions drawn from the readings.
Who is the audience?	Online audience.
How will students show their research?	A searchable website that will host everybody's research as a compilation of this history, science, and math behind natural disasters.

We can never expect more from our students without re-examining our own practices. Highly motivated students who produce high-quality, creative work require us to constantly assess whether we are assigning work that engages us or are we introducing students to learning that engages them? When making the shift, we need to keep two things buoyed in the back of our mind: what conceptual thinking do we want our students to understand? And how do we best hook and engage adolescent learners so that they are passionate about their research? Seek out that sweet spot. You'll know it when you find it!

#tldnr?

"If we want research to engage our students and jumpstart creative and critical thinking, we have to intentionally shift our assignments."

"Often, we are so concerned that our students won't find the right answers, that we provide them with so much structure they can't go wrong . . . or learn."

"When students have a voice in which direction they will explore, they will pick subjects that interest them, which will encourage them to work through the harder parts of research."

"Purpose drives the paths we take . . . It always results in intentional learning."

"Relevancy in learning is the magical congruence of what a student wants to know and what a student needs to know."

"We want research to be an autonomous act that ignites curiosity . . . Instead of asking what do we want our students to know, let's ask ourselves, what do we want them to understand?."

#tryonething

Assess one of your research projects by asking:

- What major concepts do I want students to understand?
- Is there flexibility in the topic?
- Does this assignment encourage independently drawn conclusions?
- Who is the audience?
- How will students show their research?

2

I Don't Have Time to Teach Research

Balancing Content, Skills, and Time Management

I sat down to plan a project with a teacher, and as we looked at the calendar, she asked if we could cut some steps out. "I mean, sometimes I just feel like doing research is such a time-waster," she confided.

> I could be using this time to cover my curriculum, and instead I'm using it to teach them things they should already know how to do and turn in final products that I just don't love. Can we just shorten it all up?

Let's be real: there are some herculean realities that visit and consume us daily in the classroom.

We have too many students, too many preps, too many initiatives. Our plates fill faster than we can empty them, and we devour our work with unhealthy appetites, leaving us exhausted and drained. The time we do have is forever interrupted at breathtaking accumulations, and the idea of adding one more thing, like teaching research skills, feels like filling an already-cracked bathtub with gallons of water.

Curriculum demands further intensify our job, as we try to cover all of the material expected of us. In the face of what looks like endless and impossible amounts of information we are supposed to have students successfully master, including research in our practice can look like a "time-waster."

But research doesn't have to be one more thing. And instead of a time-waster, it can become a valuable way to spend our learning time. It's shifting our practice in ways that change how our students access our content.

Content vs. Skills: It's a Marriage

In my first year of teaching, the science teacher down the hall asked me to teach the students how to take notes so they could apply it to her class. I balked at the idea—don't kids just know how to do that? You read something and then you jot down what you just learned. It seemed so simple. Why would we have to show kids how to do this?

Little did I know, we both had it wrong. Me teaching students how to take notes outside of a science class context was not an authentic method that would help students apply those skills to that content. Me not teaching them at all? That wasn't acceptable either, and I had a few years of really poor note-takers come away from my classroom. I wish we could go back and re-do that. This time I'd say—yes! I'll teach note-taking, and then I'll give you all of the language and strategies we used so that you can reiterate that instruction in your own class, because kids need to hear it more than once. We both need to be teaching skills.

This is the constant pedagogical struggle we all face, right? Do we teach skills? And if so, when? And how on earth do we teach skills while we are teaching the content that is outlined in our curricula? It is a constant worry that we cannot focus on both—skill and content—and that if we do focus on skill, we will water down and neglect content. At some point, too, we wonder (like I did in my first year), don't they have these skills already? Why do we have to keep teaching them? How can we justify the time it takes?

At the turn of the twentieth century, human knowledge was, historically, doubling every one hundred years. By the end of World War II, that number had changed to every 25 years. Generating human knowledge has accelerated over the past century, and currently, we see human knowledge double every 13 months (Schilling 2013). That is how our content grows, too—there will always be new authors to read, new wars to teach, new scientific discoveries to examine. Because knowledge is not static, we have to instead consider— how do we help students access our content?

Skills make content come alive. Close readers connect with text. Curious questioners find purpose in their learning. Organizers of information reflect on what the information says and means. When students have strong research skills, content becomes meaningful beyond memorization. Student learning becomes more efficient with the mastery of skills, and they begin to construct meaning more independently. When we teach research skills, we are sending the message—it's not about me delivering sets of facts to you; it's about you discovering your world.

Discovery Over Delivery

When my kids were younger I told them over and over again to turn their laundry right side out before they put it in the dirty pile. It's a pain for me to turn everything right side out. They would nod, say okay, and then the next day throw their shirts in with one arm inside out, jeans with legs curled up inside of one another, and socks in tiny, crispy, little balls. I would repeat my request and the laundry would continue to be put in the way that drove me crazy. I was clearly delivering and explaining the information: When you put laundry in like that it doesn't get cleaned as well and it is harder for me to fold. When they got older and began to do their own laundry, they discovered exactly what I had been lecturing about for years. Their clothes didn't come out clean and they were difficult to fold. They immediately changed their habits. Sometimes real life teaches me about my teaching practice. This time I was reminded: Delivering information is not synonymous with delivering learning, but discovery of information is the pathway to learning long-lasting lessons.

Because of the realities of our classroom, we often decide that reading, lecturing, and note-taking from the board is the most time-efficient method of learning in our classrooms. And while delivering certain information works, if we want our students to learn the real, applicable lessons, we need to allow time for discovery.

Discovery, at its roots, is connected to learning. It includes reflections, epiphanies, and failures.

Discovery is learning, and this is where research steps in. Research allows for discovery—it gives students the pathways to delve in deeper to concepts and ideas.

Research, by definition, is discovery.

Sure, any process that allows for the recursive process of learning and failing and re-attempting will take longer than delivery, but it is what connects us to the meaningful lessons.

So When Do We Let Students Discover through Research?

Deciding when students should be delving into research and determining the amount of time to dedicate to the project can be difficult. In teaching research, I have sometimes found myself spending weeks on topics that weren't deserving (think: important Medieval people) and indeed, that time felt wasted. I've also fallen into the trap where I've tried to have students come to significant conclusions in a short period of time (think: How has our political mood affected music over the course of time? You have one week: go!). Does this sound familiar? When I've struggled with this, I've found myself losing swaths of time to uninspired projects or cutting out important parts of the research process, hoping they can get it all done on their own. But all either of those situations ever resulted in were bored or frustrated students and sloppy or surface-level projects.

So when do we let students discover through research? When we want them to go deeper. When we want them to take the content we have delivered to new levels that personalize, extend, and explore. When we want them to apply concepts to their own worlds. In short, as often as we can.

We can determine whether we want students to embark on long research projects or small research tasks by considering the objectives of the unit or lesson. Smaller research projects are better for uncovering background information, while larger projects are better for end-of-unit, synthesis of information.

Small Research Projects

Not every research project has to even be a "project" or end with a culminating, polished piece. In fact, shorter, on-the-spot research endeavors are perfect for targeting and reinforcing specific skills. For example, in Heather Belanger's US History II class, we co-teach a one-week terrorism unit. We have two sets of goals: curriculum goals and research goals. The end curriculum goal is for students to understand the causes of terrorism and to write an essay answering the question, "Why does terrorism exist and what should the world be doing about it?" The research goals are to reinforce searching, assessing, and note-taking skills.

Students each choose a major terrorist organization that piques their interest and then, every day, we present students with a question to drive their fact-finding. Questions like: *What is the organization's primary mission? How does recruitment occur? What training practices are used?*

As our students find answers during the first part of class, they keep track of valid and credible sources, and use note cards to write down notes. For the second half of class, we sit in a circle and discuss everyone's findings and compare and contrast the information. We watch Season 3, Episode 1 of "The West Wing" and they fact check the information they viewed. We listen to podcasts about empathy, enemies, and roots of terrorism. They turn in their notes and sources daily and we spend a few minutes at the end of class perusing them, assessing quality and credibility. By the end of the end of the week, they have more information about terrorist organization structures than we could ever have given them, in the same amount of time. This is the beauty of discovery.

Short research undertakings like this do not eat into our curriculum time, they reinforce skills for larger assignments, they make research a habit, and there is no gargantuan, culminating project at the end of each day.

Larger Research Projects

That isn't to say that larger project don't have their place. When deciding when to incorporate these into the classroom, think conceptually. What major themes and concepts do you want students to understand about a particular unit of study? These are good times for students to delve into issues and topics of their choice and apply it to that concept. In Heather Clogston's Early Childhood Development class, she wants students to understand underlying issues that affect young children. In a semester-long research project, students identify early on an issue that they are interested in. We meet for half periods, two to three days a week, chunking the research into bite-size pieces, slowing down the process, and giving students time to really delve into and consider an issue of their choice, while applying the content covered throughout the semester. As a culminating project, each student writes and presents a mini-TED talk, so that every class member is exposed to the information in an engaging, interesting way.

Long-term research projects run more successfully when the required skills are practiced routinely in smaller doses and work best when student-centered inquiry can pull larger concepts together, granting students the opportunity to apply and make meaning of knowledge.

If we go back to my five underlying beliefs about teaching research to guide us in research instruction, we can begin to combat the normal pitfalls that often bog us down in the research process:

- **Research helps students make meaning of their world.**
  It also helps students make meaning of your content. Given opportunities to delve into choice-driven, relevant topics, students will apply their learning to the larger concepts you want them to understand.

- **Research is an act of citizenship.**
  Certainly, we want students to make informed decisions in their lives, but we also want them to make informed decisions in our classrooms. Students who know how to read for bias and assess resources will be more positive contributors to our classroom conversations.

- **Research skills are explicitly taught in every discipline.**
  By providing explicit instruction—giving students strategies like the ones in this book to access, assess, organize, and use information, we help them manage their time more wisely. While it takes time to teach these skills, it helps them use their time in the classroom more efficiently, paying off in the end.

- **Research becomes a habit.**
  Integrating smaller projects with larger ones reinforces specific skills, so that when students take on larger projects they are, again, using their time more efficiently. One-shot deals aren't enough for mastery of complex thinking skills. In each section of this book, models of long and short projects for each skill will be given. As research becomes more integrated in the classroom, better quality final products become the result.

- **Research is an act of creation.**
  Assignments that invite the creation of knowledge and new findings will have higher quality results. By making sure that we are explicitly teaching research skills, we will help with time management. Smaller deadlines along the way assist students in the pacing of a longer research project. And when we incorporate shorter, more focused research projects that do not have large culminating final products, students can master the skills for larger projects, making them the kind of quality we all hope for.

But the Time!

If there is anything middle and high school students are excellent at, it is wasting time. I am certain that I am not the only teacher who has given students an entire period or two or three (or a week!) to research a topic only to find that they have a few piddly facts scribbled down. I'm further certain that I'm not the only teacher whose students find they don't have enough information and turn in subquality and surface-level work that has clearly been done the night (or lunch period) before. I've seen it in every discipline, at every grade level I've taught.

But one day, something very interesting occurred that made me realize we need to teach our students how to use their time. Another teacher and I, who co-teach an independent action research/capstone project class together, started class with a quick impromptu research project. Each student drew a card from Apples to Apples and had 30 minutes to find information about the topic, and put together a meaningful presentation.

And they did. In fact, they pulled together projects that were of the same (or better!) quality than what we had seen students turn in after a week's worth of work.

We then gave them a list of deadlines for the semester-long, intensive project that they were about to undertake and modeled the first piece of note-taking and had them get to work. But they didn't. They clicked on sites. They watched some relevant videos. They went to the bathroom. They talked about their mornings. And after a few days of independent note-taking they had a few things marked down, but nothing that looked like three days' worth of hard work. I thought back to that initial 30 minutes when they were so productive.

What was going wrong? These students were productive one day and not the next. We sat and talked about it and realized: we haven't explicitly helped students understand how to use their time.

Sometimes we think that if we help older kids structure their time, we are holding their hands. But instead, we should view it as a metacognitive practice that guides their progress, allowing them to feel the success that comes with timely work completion. Explicit instruction in how to manage time results in higher productivity in our classrooms. This is a lesson we all can use over and over again.

Here are some ways we can help our students learn how to manage their time:

- Do the 30-minute challenge. Have students draw a card with a random topic on it and research and present. This sets the groundwork for productivity. It opens up a discussion about how they used their time and what worked for them.

- Do a 5-minute challenge. In some classes, we have done a shorter version of this: students read resources that are relevant to their current topic of research and take notes for 5 minutes, and then in 5 more minutes pull together a quick visual presentation. After this task, I have had students say that they want to work for 5-minute bursts with a 1- or 2-minute break between. I have had students say that they couldn't believe that they could actually learn so much in 5 minutes. Sometimes they just need to be shown what they are truly capable of.

- When delving into a longer project or paper, ask students what they envision at the end—what do they hope their final product will be or look like? What kind of quality are they shooting for? And then ask them what steps they need to take to make that happen. Often, students know what they want something to be, but require conversation to determine how to actually get there.

- Have students self-structure their class time. Instead of saying, "You have the next 45 minutes to take notes," ask them, "What do you need to accomplish today?" and have them jot that down on a notecard. Some kids may make a checklist; some may write a quick narrative. At the end of the class period, have them reflect on the back of their notecard how successful they were and why or why not and have them report to one another. It's a twist on the exit form.

- Use calendars. Have students list all the steps they need to take and then give them a calendar and the time to plug those steps into the different time periods they have. What can they get done in class? What do they need to do at home? Check in frequently on progress and hold them accountable for meeting these self-designated deadlines.

Many students will say "I need to take notes" or "I need to read." Challenge them to write more specific tasks. *What do you need to take notes on? What specifically do you need to read? How much?* Direct them to really think about what needs to be accomplished in the time they have and to write qualitative daily goals. This explicit time management instruction benefits our students long term—they learn strategies to complete work in a timely manner and they feel the confidence that comes with turning in work they are proud of without the stress of rushing in the end. And while taking the time out of our content instruction to work on these skills may feel like adding "one more thing," we will discover instead that the quality and quantity of work accomplished in our classrooms improves.

Remember, our students' brains are still developing—even our most advanced high school students—and if none of us works with time and skill, we are failing to help them build the necessary neural pathways that will help them manage their time independently in college and life. It can start with an Apples to Apples topic, a calendar, a timer, and an index card.

But What about *Our* Time? Planning and Managing a Project

"If everybody is researching something different—something that they picked—my classroom will likely dissolve into chaos," a teacher confided in me at a conference. "I mean, I have 30 kids in a class. There is no way I can plan, let alone keep on top of that. What you are suggesting feels pie-in-the-sky impossible."

This is real. Planning for individualized instruction looms intimidatingly large. Furthermore, most of us do have 20–25 students in a classroom and being caught up on everything is a rare event. However, with a few organizational tools, it doesn't have to be chaotic or impossible.

Planning

Many of us read Wiggins and McTighe's *Understanding By Design* years ago for a course we took. If you have it, dust it off and revisit it—because it's such a help when designing research projects. The premise of UBD is backwards planning—to think of where you want to be and then work towards that. It breaks it down into three parts:

1. Identifying desired results
2. Determining assessment and evidence
3. Planning learning experiences

Without planning backwards, we can fall into many pitfalls. Our assessments may not align with our initial goals. The relevancy to the research may lose momentum. Students may be unclear of their purpose. And it may begin to take so long that we skip important pieces of the process. So what does backwards planning look like when planning out a research project?

Identifying Desired Results	Determining Assessment and Evidence	Planning Learning Experiences
• What are my main research objectives? • What are my main content objectives? • What concepts do I want students to understand? • What is the essential question (if I am providing it)? • How do I want students to be able to transfer their knowledge?	• What do I want students to produce in the end? • How can students explain, interpret, and apply what they learn meaningfully? • How much time will this take?	• What resources will students need from me? • Which mini-lessons will help them progress independently? • What steps do students need to arrive at the final goal? • Does the time needed for this align with the time I can give?

After framing your thoughts for the project, creating a calendar that helps map out the project is beneficial. Be realistic and incorporate class time and any intended homework time. If the project seems too big for that timeline, consider scale. One week to research, write, and produce a video is not enough time, but it might be enough time to research and write a few paragraphs, contribute to a debate, or create a small poster.

Managing

Keeping track of 25–30 teenagers can be hard! But with the proper organizational tools, it is not impossible. Here are some ways to keep creativity alive, personalization thrumming, and your sanity reigned in all at once:

Daily Slips

Ask students to set their personalized agenda for the class period. As you move around the room to meet with students, you can use those to focus them and help push them towards higher productivity and success. When they walk in and start their day with a "to-do" list they will be more productive than when they walk in and "research." Be clear about what small steps go into the bigger steps, so they can be more specific about what they need to do (i.e. instead of saying "take notes" they can say "finish the notes about Thomas Jefferson's philosophy on slavery").

At the end of class, provide them with the time and space to reflect on what was accomplished and what they need to do next.

Conference Sheets

The conference sheet is the godsend to individualized research organization. Create a sheet for each student that has his or her name, topic, and thesis at the top. Each day you meet with the student, take notes. These notes will help you remember what was said, what the student was struggling with, and where that student needs to go next. If co-teaching, conference sheets are great records of what the other teacher has said, so that you can continue to support and augment one another's work. Stapling daily slips to the back of the conference sheet provides a record of student work.

Research Step Sheets

Somewhere in the classroom, hang up pieces of paper (or draw on a board) the different steps of the research process. Give students stickers, have them draw an avatar, or ask them to use a first initial to sign off each time they complete a step in the process. This helps students see where they are at in the larger scheme of things. My experience, also, is that those students who are not performing by choice often pick up their speed when they visually see that everybody else is progressing without them.

Developing your own organizational system is key to success in the independent research. Whatever method you choose, if you ensure that students can articulate what needs to be done every step of the way and you have a record of each conversation, the chaos and loss of control that makes us fearful will dissipate.

REFLECTION SHEET

Name: _____ Date: _____

Today's goal:

What I need to do to be successful:

Topic:

Here's what I accomplished today and how I feel about that:

Next step:

eRESOURCES

SAMPLE CONFERENCE SHEET

Name: Sophie

Topic: Racism/To Kill a Mockingbird

Working thesis:
Even though we think TKAM is history, if we look closely at modern society, we haven't come as far as we'd like to think.

Date	Conference Notes	What's Next
4/3	Chose three subtopics: housing/legal segregation; police brutality/racial profiling; prejudicial discrimination.	Start to read about subtopics.
4/6	Conversation about Freddie Gray. Re-read NYT article and brainstormed some more questions.	Continue reading.
4/7	Talked about similarities between how Tom is treated and how African Americans are treated re: news articles.	Start taking notes on information that has been found.
4/10	Trouble with understanding some of the information—talked through articles.	Continue note-taking.
4/11	Notes for AA/police taken; moving on to housing segregation. Listening to NPR podcast.	Listen to podcast; take notes; find more resources.
. . .	. . .	. . .

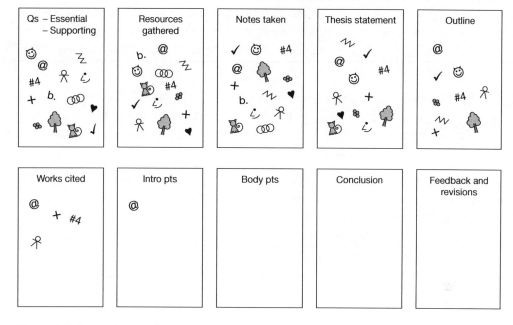

Figure 2.1 Research step sheets

TAKING A CLOSER LOOK

Rachel Bartlett

Science

Rachel Bartlett, a 7th grade science teacher who has also taught high school, understands that when students have mastered skills, they can master her content. In the beginning of the year she does a one-week unit on confirmation bias. She wants her students to acknowledge that we all have biases and the role those biases play when examining scientific data. Confirmation bias is a little more complex—in confirmation bias, we glean information, read and interpret data, dismiss statistics, or just push a little to make things say what we want. This is obviously a troublesome practice in science. Her Confirmation Bias unit is a model of how research skills like assessing credibility and summarizing can be taught to augment academic skills.

Rachel tells me,

> I start the unit by having students read two articles: one saying climate change is real; the other saying it isn't, both using data to prove their points. We then do a close reading activity where students pull apart and break down the data, assessing its

credibility. They draw conclusions that the points made in the "Climate Change Is Not Real" article either do not have data to support them or it pulls small pieces of data from long-term collections, making it unreliable. They quickly realize—this is what bias looks like.

The following day, students move around to different stations, reading case studies, looking at cartoons, and taking part in small experiments to solidify their understanding of why and how confirmation bias exists. By the end of that class, they are ready to apply their knowledge.

Students then spend time on ProCon.org looking for science issues that are relevant to their lives or that they are interested in. Topics like—Are vaccinations safe? Should animals be used for experimentation? Is vegetarianism a preferred diet? Should we use alternative energy? Are cell phones safe? They take a stance and find data that supports their stance. But then they have to pull data that supports the other side. From this point on, they are in an internal struggle—which data was the correctly used data?

In the end, students draw cartoons or write paragraphs that show how data could be used to support both arguments. Starting the year like this is powerful—they have the mindset to assess data and think like critical scientists. But what surprises me most is that they began to apply this understanding of confirmation bias to their greater world—politics, school issues, the news. When students have research skills, they are savvy learners.

#tldnr?

"It is a constant worry that we cannot focus on both—skill and content—and that if we do focus on skill, we will water down and neglect content."

"Because knowledge is not static, we have to instead consider—how do we help students access our content?"

"Skills make content come alive."

"If we want students to learn the real, applicable lessons, we need to allow time for discovery . . . research, by definition, is discovery."

"So when do we let students discover through research? When we want them to take the content we have delivered to new levels that personalize, extend, and explore."

"Explicit instruction in how to manage time results in higher productivity in our classrooms."

#tryonething

Do a quick study of student productivity.

Try the 30-minute challenge. Have students randomly draw an Apples to Apples topic card and then give them 30 minutes to research and come up with a visual presentation. This sets the groundwork for productivity. It opens up a discussion about how they used their time and what worked for them, and allows you to see their potential under the gun!

3

Finding Focus

Using Presearch and Questioning to Narrow and Refine Research

When I first stepped into the classroom, teaching research felt like an act of chaos that I tried to rein in with rigid checklists and processes. But no matter what attempt I made to bring deliberate control to the process, the work that was handed in routinely disappointed me because it often felt too broad or too specific. I read papers about the Civil War, condensed into five pages. I read three-page papers about Aruba. I read papers about the Ku Klux Klan. Yes, the formatting was correct, they were proofread, and a variety of sources were used, but these research papers weren't saying anything meaningful, and I didn't know how to help students find focus. When I confessed to a group of students that I needed assistance in helping them become better researchers, Lily, a girl in the back row, spoke up and said, "My writing is so boring I don't even want to proofread it. I just don't care."

I looked at the entire class, and they all slowly nodded their heads. "Okay." I took a deep breath. "What can we do then?" The class sat silently for a few minutes before students started contributing. Slowly, two ideas ultimately emerged:

1. We do not know enough to choose a topic that is interesting or that has enough resources.
2. There is no point to what we're writing. We're just paraphrasing what somebody else has said.

What my students were identifying was the need to develop focus. After that conversation, we scrapped the paper we were working on and started over, implementing two important missing pieces: Presearch and Questioning.

Presearch

Sometimes we give students a list of topics to study and sometimes we give them complete choice. (We'll talk about the paths of inquiry offered to students later in this chapter.) We tell them to "pick a topic" or to "brainstorm ideas," but often forget to unpack those terms for them. Brainstorming and choosing a direction takes time and should start with what I call *presearch*: dedicated time for exploration. Let me introduce the idea by telling you about Alex's experience with presearch.

We were well into a research project, when I sat down to conference with Alex in the library and asked him how the writing process for his research paper was going. "Surprisingly well," he responded. I stopped with my pen midair and looked up, slightly astounded, because this young man was frequently cynical and rarely answered my questions with positivity. "How's the *quality* of the writing?" I inquired. "Better than decent," he modestly declared. When I asked him why this was going so well and if we could pinpoint what exactly was making his writing strong, he said, "Honestly? It's because you gave me time to explore. I actually know and like my topic."

Alex was right. We *had* given him time to explore. We had instituted presearch into our initial instruction—a practice that allows students time to simply peruse gathered books, articles, databases, and Internet sources, while looking for a topic that is of high interest to them.

I had worked with Alex on previous assignments, where presearch had not been included. Each time he had either been assigned a topic or quickly and compliantly chosen one. He had started collecting material, but then, lost steam. Each time his interest in the topic waned, and eventually he declared that he just didn't care. Most times he didn't even finish the assignment, or what he did turn in was uninspired and late. Alex, like Drew, like Lily, had a difficult time caring, and because of that, had a difficult time following through and creating quality material.

This time, though, was different. Alex was interested and invested and was writing and producing something he was excited about.

The Importance of Exploration

Too often we ask students to choose topics and start taking notes all within the same class period. As teachers, we always feel that insistent and inevitable pressure of needing to move forward and not waste time, and it's hard to justify an entire class period where nothing more tangible than an idea is produced. We worry that if we give students time to just peruse the Internet, they will waste it, because the reality is, middle and high schoolers can be masters of wasting unstructured class time.

But when students understand that we are doing this because it empowers them—that we are tying their autonomy to their research—they find immense benefit to the process and use their time wisely. "We are usually asked to choose a topic," one student said to me,

> but we don't even know what kinds of topics are interesting. We haven't read anything yet. We don't know *anything*, so we just pick *something*. And then if we change our minds, we're in too far and will fall behind.

This student was absolutely right. Presearch allows students to get comfortable with a topic. But it goes beyond just finding something: If they can't talk about a topic, they aren't able to build questions. If they can't build questions, they won't be able to formulate a productive search. If they can't formulate a productive search, they won't be able to find good sources. Presearch is, ultimately, the keystone, to an effective research project.

When students are given time to explore, their research becomes driven by their curiosity, and we know that the best research takes place when we are genuinely curious. Fewer students switch topics, and nobody chooses a topic for which there are not enough sources readily available. The initial investment of time prepares them to utilize the remaining time better.

Dr. Carol Kuhlthau, a research professor at Rutgers University, clumps the phases of research into two categories: Exploration and Collection. The Exploration phase is when students get to do their presearch—they "dip" into the topic, rather than "dig" in. The Collection phase comes later when they start to gather resources.

We know the world is round because of adventurous explorers who took off to find the ends of the world in ships. We know that radiation causes cancer because of scientific explorers who sacrificed their own health to their studies. We know that empathy is the root of tolerance because of research explorers who have been willing to venture into the uncomfortable situations of humanity. We know what exists miles under the ocean because of diving explorers who immerse themselves into the unknown waters that cover our earth. We know that exploration is the root of all learning.

If we make exploration an intrinsic piece of the research processes, we help ensure successful student discovery and success.

There are numerous benefits to integrating presearch exploration into the process.

- The practice of explorative thinking benefits neurological pathways. When we ask students to immerse themselves in presearch, we are asking them to wander intellectually, a process that is a different kind of thinking and needs lots of practice. This is important work for their brains that becomes reinforced with practice.

- Exploration increases creativity. People who have original and creative ideas do not necessarily have better ideas—they just have more. And they don't usually go with their first idea (Grant 2016). In fact, first ideas tend to be the most conventional and conservative ones, so when we give students the time and space to peruse, discuss, and brainstorm, we are allowing them the time and space to be original and creative. Creativity can be taught by encouraging students to stand out, not fit into a mold (Barras 2014), and so we need to allow them ways to shape their own research. Presearch is the initial step.

- Exploration allows students to make sure they have adequate resources. We have all seen students choose a topic they're wild about, only to find that there is not enough information for them to collect, and then fall behind as they struggle with gathering resources, only to change topics to something that they are half-hearted about, in the end. When students know that viability is part of exploration, they are more flexible in finding alternative topics. They learn that the failures of exploration do not define them.

- Students are more invested in what they are studying when exploration is included in their research practices. By being able to shed uninteresting topics and spend time getting to know the topics that interest them, they are more likely to stay the course with their chosen topic.

- Presearch better prepares students to build research questions and search effectively with content-specific vocabulary.

What Presearch Looks Like

Step One

Pull together appropriate resources from the library and online for them to peruse. These resources will be jumping points for students to get ideas from. In a 1920s unit I co-teach, we pull together a research guide (I use a Springhare product, LibGuides) with articles on everything from music to the Great Depression to immigration to Harlem to photography. We find entire sites on the 1920s from places like the History Channel, PBS, the National Archives, Life Magazine, etc. We dump piles of library books in front of them, free for the taking and perusing. We resist offering them a list of ideas, because while this seems like a help, it is actually counterintuitive—it often restricts their thinking and does not encourage original or creative thought. It's like keeping them on the tourist-line boardwalks in Yellowstone. We'd rather they find that "unbeaten path" and meander down it.

Step Two

Set a rule of silence—this is not the time to discuss with classmates (yet!). Right now it's about focusing, and settling into independent inquiry.

Step Three

Give students an entire period to explore independently. Explain to them,

> If it's boring you, turn the page or click out of it. And pay attention to what grabs your attention. Which topics are leading you on trails—which titles are making you dig further? What's really cool? That's where you want to land. That's the gateway to your topic. Today isn't about taking notes or starting a presentation—it's simply about losing yourself to something interesting. When you find yourself quiet, leaning in, asking yourself questions, wanting to know more, jotting down new words, you know you've found your topic.

Step Four

Step back. Let them explore.

Step Five

Start navigating the room to have brief, quiet conversations with students. Ask them questions like:

- What are you finding?
- What are you passionate about?

- What do you want to know more about?
- What resources have been helpful to you?

Help them by suggesting search terms and new ideas, but not definitive topics. Use your expertise and your librarian to connect their interests with the content. Starting sentences with, "If you like _____, you might be interested in _____" is a good way to direct them to new ideas without removing the autonomy from their search.

After Exploration: Narrowing the Focus

After students have had a chance to peruse a variety of resources and have some ideas as to what kinds of topics they want to delve into, it's time for them to start thinking about narrowing the scope of their possibilities. This was an important step I was missing back in my early days of teaching, and the reason why students handed in five pages that summarized the entire Civil War. Narrowing a focus is difficult for most students, because it takes prior knowledge. If you don't know anything about the Civil War, but are curious, how do you pick a topic that you own and are invested in? Presearch offers students the opportunity to build sufficient prior knowledge to build the autonomy necessary for focused, independent and curiosity-driven research. This step makes it easier for them. This is also the time when peer conversation and sharing becomes helpful. There are several different ways I do this in our classrooms.

Brainswarming

Brainswarming, a term coined in a *Harvard Business Review* article by Tony McCaffrey, applies swarm theory—the concept that individual actions can add up to complex ideas and behaviors—to address the goals of brainstorming —coming up with viable and creative ideas. In brainswarming, ideas are collected and shared out to a larger group and then expanded upon through crowd-sourcing. While originally intended for business gatherings, it is an effective way for students to use one another to find focus. In brainstorming, we ask students to individually come up with, refine, and proceed with an idea. Often, this leads to the commitment to one singular, conforming idea. In brainswarming, however, we offer an authentic collaborative environment where our ideas grow and flourish because of others' contributions. There are several quick and easy ways to include brainswarming into your classroom.

Sticky-note Swarm

- Each student writes their research ideas on a sticky note (one idea per note) and places them on a shared surface (like a wall or a whiteboard) as they browse through their initial resources.

- Students circulate and read what others have already posted as they go along and either leave questions, comments, or "me too's" on other sticky notes.

- Students move the sticky notes to clumps so that they are categorized. The board becomes fluid, and the ideas start to build upon one another, so that students start to see different suggestions to their original topic choices.

Students benefit by using one another's strengths and ideas to flesh out topics through safe sticky-note-conversations.

Card Pass Around Swarm

Crowdsourcing is indeed a powerful tool. With index cards, we can institute another form of it in this process.

- Hand out index cards.

- Students write down their topic ideas.

- Collect the cards, shuffle them, and then pass them back to everyone so that nobody knows who has had which idea.

- From there, students do what they did with the sticky notes— write questions or add comments to enhance the ideas or to help flesh out their own ideas.

- Have everyone pass the cards to the right or you can collect, shuffle, and re-hand out. Do this three or four times, and everybody gets a card back with new ideas on the topic.

Writing Swarm

Writing is thinking, so if students have a chance to write before they share out, it provides opportunity for everybody, not just those who process quickly and are verbally articulate, to prepare equally.

- Students do a quickwrite reflecting on the feasibility and scope of their topic idea.

- After writing for a few minutes, students share with the person next to them.

- Each student shares to the entire group topic ideas that their partner has. This allows students to hear their ideas verbalized.

- Other students can then add their questions, comments, or ideas to the discussion.

Musical Chairs Feedback Swarm

Another form of brainswarming and storming integrates writing, movement, and conversation.

- Students write their topic ideas on a large piece of paper and leave it on a desk or table in one minute.

- You play music or set a timer (students prefer music—even the seniors!).

- Students then play a "musical chairs" game of sorts, moving around the room until you stop the timer or music or ring a bell.

- Students go to the closest paper to them, read the topic, and then write down any questions/ideas they have about that topic for another 30 seconds.

- They then move again and do this for several pieces of paper.

We have also done this verbally, where when the music stops or the bell rings, they grab the person closest to them and share out their ideas with one another.

Moving Forward

No matter which kind of brainswarm you want your students to do (and after reading these, you may have come up with your own variation!), we are always asking students to really think about what they want to learn about.

- Why is their topic *important*?
- What is the *purpose*?
- Is there *enough information?*
- Is the *topic appropriate for the size of the project and the time given*?

We want students to be able to define their direction as comprehensively as possible before we move forward into the question-asking phase, where they will solidify their course of research.

Questions: What if They Ask the Wrong Ones?

Heather's Story

A few years ago, Heather, a new health teacher to our school, approached me about scheduling some library research time for her class to work on a mental illness research project. The students arrived with a list of 20 questions to answer. Questions like: How many people suffer from the disease? What are the symptoms? When do symptoms appear? What are the treatments?

I showed the students our databases and health resource book collection, and provided them with a list of high-quality websites like mentalhealth.gov and the National Association of Mental Illness and the National Institute of Mental Health. But instead of using the excellent resources at hand, the students opened Google and typed in, "How many people suffer from schizophrenia?" They looked for the answers and immediately plunked the fact down into a PowerPoint slide.

As they went through the process, I sat with them and asked them other questions about their topic. Questions like, "What is surprising about this?" or "Is there any stigma to this illness?" And they stared at me blankly. "That's not on our sheet," one answered, before going back to Google.

After the project was over, Heather sat to reflect on the project with me. She confessed that the final projects did not meet her expectations. She worried that the students had not really learned the severity of mental illness, nor did they understand the impact mental illness has on the quality of life. She found the final products to be presentations that entailed students reading lists of facts to their classmates and not thoughtful presentations of ideas supported by facts.

The following quarter when she approached me about taking on the same project, I asked her what she thought about students developing their own questions instead of giving them a list of predetermined questions to answer. She looked at me hesitantly and asked, "But what if they don't come up with the right ones?"

I understand this fear. We are obligated to guide students through particular curriculum, and there is immense pressure to cover all of the material. If we provide them with a list of what they need to look up, we can ensure that it is all covered—thoroughly and quickly. However, there is danger in this scripted question-providing practice. While students *can and will* look up material, they *will not* analyze or synthesize that material in any way. My principal said to our staff recently,

> If students can Google the answers to your assignments, then you need to consider what you are asking them to do. Do you want them to be able to Google answers? Or do you want them to be able to think?

When we provide students with lists of Google-able questions, we are not encouraging independent thinking, because we've already done the thinking for them.

The following quarter, Heather and I approached the project differently. We asked students to presearch and find a mental illness that they were interested in. We discovered that most chose a topic that was closely related to them or a loved one. We then asked them to formulate an essential question—a question that they wanted to answer that couldn't be Googled. Students came up with questions like *How do we support friends who have social anxiety? Are we doing enough for schizophrenia in our society? Do schools support students with depression?* From there, students developed supporting questions and developed miniTED talks that answered their essential question. The result? Students not only covered the material she had hoped they would, but well-surpassed her expectations. Students made meaningful and powerful presentations that engaged and inspired their peers and generated excellent post-presentation conversations. By simply shifting the control of questioning to the students, the quality of the research was raised.

Every teacher longs for empowered students who are active learners and critical thinkers. For this to happen, we need to shift to models like Heather's class, where creating is promoted over consuming (Wagner 2015). When students develop their own questions, they initiate their own thinking, pairing curiosity and connection and are more invested in their learning. Asking questions helps develop a set of skills that leads to intentional learning. But more importantly, questioning can increase awe and wonder, and with awe and wonder comes deep, meaningful learning.

So What's Next? Understanding Questions

Coming up with good questions is the most important part of focusing our students' research experience. Because of this, there are entire books written about the art, science, and pedagogy of developing good questions, and I recommend reading these if you are struggling with developing questions— they are every bit worth your time. But for the sake of simplicity, pragmatism, and immediately implementable practice, let's unpack questioning in concrete student terms.

Breaking questions up into two kinds is a concrete, easily understandable way to teach questioning to students: there are essential questions and supporting questions.

Essential Questions

This is what I tell my students as I draw a thought cloud on the board, when they are embarking on a research project:

The essential question is the big question you want to answer for this project. It is not a Google-able question. It requires you to read a bunch of material and then think about what you've learned and create your own answers.

For essential questions, we synthesize. That means we look at a lot of different material and draw our own conclusions. We come up with our own answers based on what we've learned. We're not just repeating what somebody else has researched.

Essential questions need to be open-ended, not closed—that means they need to have answers that are not right or wrong. They need to have answers that require explanations.

Think about conversations you have with your parents. If you go home and say you did poorly on an assignment, and they ask, "Did you study?" you are going to give them a one-word answer: yes. They didn't ask you an open-ended question. But if they ask, "Why do you think you did poorly?" they are now asking you to think about your studying, your preparation, your understanding of what you learned. They are asking you to synthesize all of that information and pull it together to draw conclusions. That is an open-ended question.

So as you think about developing an essential research question, think about— what do you really want to know? What are the big ideas that you want to get at? Sometimes starting those questions with "how" or "why" helps. Thinking of comparing things helps. Thinking of how causes affect later events helps. But remember—you won't know the answer to this question until you have done all of your research.

This is certainly an oversimplified version of what an essential question actually is, but when teaching it to students, I am more interested in how they can access the task. This conversation acts as a launching pad for students to jump into questioning successfully.

A social studies teacher I work with has her students write their essential question on a shared Google Doc so that they can all see each others' and use those examples as models. She and I then go in and give feedback and suggestions. Usually students need a couple of drafts and a conversation with one of us until they have a viable research question.

McTighe and Wiggins, two leaders in developing questionings, emphasize that when students are writing their own essential question, intention trumps form (2013). I think this is important to remember. As long as you and the student know what they want to know, don't worry about if it is phrased sophisticatedly. Sometimes my students' essential questions are very awkwardly phrased, but through conversation, I can tell that they know what they want to know. Essential questions drive the research, so the researcher is the one who needs to know the intention. As long as they have a clear direction and genuine curiosity, I do not push to have a finely phrased question. I let intention trump form every time.

Supporting Questions

Having students develop their essential question is not enough to focus their research. They have to understand that there are smaller, more concrete questions they need to answer in order to get to their final answer. Supporting questions scaffold the research they need to do. Asking students to backwards-design their research by developing supporting questions helps them see a clearer path for their research. This is what I tell them:

If your essential question is what comes from your head—is a synthesis of all the material you read—how do you know what to look up? Some of these topics have entire books or encyclopedia sets written about them. That can be really overwhelming. You will have to narrow your reading by creating a list of supporting questions.

Supporting questions are your right-there-look-up questions. They are your facts, your numbers, your dates and events, your people, your places, your timelines. They are the data you need to collect to synthesize for that final, big question. So I'm going to ask you to plan backwards a little bit. You know where you want to be in the end—that final big question. But what do you need to know to get there? Step all the way back and look at that whole picture. What data do you need to collect?

These questions are going to guide you as you research. It doesn't mean you won't find other information that is important. You may even find that as you go along new questions pop up. That's okay! Let them! Add them to your list!

As much as possible, I try to model every step of the research process with my students. So during this entire conversation, I come up with an essential question on the board and then talk my way through developing supporting questions. By modeling the process, we make the thinking transparent and accessible. We also let them see that sometimes we are inarticulate. That sometimes our questions have to change. That coming to terms with questioning can be a messy process and that's okay.

Supporting Student-generated Questions

One day, while working with a group of teachers on unpacking standards, the subject of student-generated essential questions came up. One teacher leaned in, and said, "I mean, really. Do we even *want* students to be asking their own questions?"

Asking questions builds knowledge while also personalizing the learning experience. Good questions launch the framework of good research, and the more questions students ask, the better they get. And most importantly, curiosity is the root of excellent inquiry.

In brief, yes. Yes we do want students to be asking their own questions.

But just asking students to develop questions isn't enough. Using the visual of the pictures of the thought bubble and the book are certainly ways to concretely depict the differences between essential and supporting questions, but many students need scaffolded practice to develop their own essential questions. When scaffolding, think of it as a four-step, metacognitive process:

1. **Generating**—Students come up with as many questions as they can. They get their juices flowing!

2. **Categorizing**—Students determine which of their questions are open-ended and which are closed. This is a step towards the development of the essential question

3. **Prioritizing**—Students think about which questions are most important to them.

4. **Improving**—Students fine-tune their focus and build the question they are most excited about.

This is what I tell students when they are ready to develop their questions:

Generating
Write as many questions as you can think of. Don't judge them as "good questions" or "bad questions." Just write! Don't hyper-analyze yourself. Don't second-guess yourself. Just write down as many questions as you can. Our best ideas rarely come out the first time.

Categorizing
Now, look at all of those questions. Which ones are open-ended? That means they need lots of different information to explain. Which ones are closed? That means they have "right there" Google-able answers. Find a way to label them—circle them, highlight them, check them . . . but ultimately, pull out those open-ended questions.

Prioritizing
Now, look at those open-ended questions. Which ones speak to you the most? Which ones are overarching for your close-ended questions? Which one makes you the most curious? Can any of them be combined?

Improving
In this step, you're going to really think about those questions. Why is this important or interesting to you? What do you want to know or do? How do you hope to find information for this? It's not enough to just ask *questions, you have to think about what comes behind that question. I want you to remember—that if it's awkwardly phrased, that's okay. Your intention trumps your form. Meaning, what you want from the question is much more important than if you've used the most precise words.*

When students approach the task of question-developing from a meta-cognitive standpoint, they are empowered to drive their own learning in powerful ways.

But What About Teacher-generated Questions?
There are times when teachers understandably want to pose a teacher-generated essential question for students to research—we want them to really investigate a piece of the curriculum or use their collective research to contribute to a whole-class discussion. We want inquiry-based units where students are researching to find the answers to the bigger questions we have. Posing a question does not necessarily indicate research in class is happening though.

To understand where teacher-generated questions come into the classroom, let's have a conversation about inquiry-based learning. Most of our standards—Common Core, other state standards, Next Generation Science Standards, and the C3 History Standards all call for a shift to inquiry-based learning.

Inquiry-based classrooms are driven by questions rather than the presentation of information. There are four levels of inquiry: structured, controlled, guided, and free. Structured is solely teacher-centered, where the teacher poses a question and provides a whole-class resource. Free inquiry is entirely student-centered, where students design their own questions and find their own resources. Controlled and guided inquiry are the stepping stones from teacher-centered inquiry to student-centered inquiry. The terms inquiry and research often get confused and some use them interchangeably, but I'd like to propose a new way to think about inquiry.

If inquiry is thought of as question-asking, it does not necessarily have to include research. Questions that can be answered by provided texts, questions that have definitive right or wrong answers, questions that are supported by further teacher-generated questions do not require research skills for answering. Real research involves asking questions, finding and assessing resources, and synthesizing to draw conclusions. If the questions and the resources are provided, and the conclusions have a right or wrong answer, students are fact-finding, not researching.

But research should include inquiry, especially student-generated inquiry. The very word itself—*inquiry*— carries the connotation of discovery, excitement, and curiosity. Students who are inquisitive are looking for new ways to learn. They are passionate. For me, inquiry means probing, searching, speculating, investigating. I connect inquiry with being filled with wonder and as the driving force behind research—it makes us ask big questions and seek out satisfying answers.

For the sake of this book then, which is about research—that complex act of looking for answers from multiple perspectives—we are going to focus on guided and free inquiry processes, because when students are involved with the development of their questions, their purposes for learning become authentic. In guided inquiry, teachers provide the essential question, but students develop the supporting questions to guide their searches. In open inquiry, students take the helm and develop their essential and supporting questions. Putting inquiry and question-asking into the hands of our students shifts their inquiry to research.

Teacher-generated Essential Questions

When generating our own essential questions for students, we want to keep in mind two things:

- Questions are broad enough for students to generate knowledge, rather than repeat or recall facts.
- Questions are open and overarching—there is no right or wrong answer.

TEACHER-GENERATED ESSENTIAL QUESTIONS	
There are a thousand ways to start questions, but below are some new ways to think about designing teacher-generated questions, followed by cross-content examples to get the juices flowing!	
Question Stems	**Sample Questions**
Based on . . . what can you predict about . . .?	*Based on two different mathematical climate change models, what different predictions can we make about the earth's surface?* *Based on the decrease of OPEC production and the rise of American oil, what can be predicted about gas prices?*
What are the differences between . . . and . . .?	*How did media coverage in the Vietnam War differ from coverage in previous wars?* *What are the differences between schizophrenia and borderline personality disorder?*
How are . . . and . . . similar?	*How are Brexit, the 2016 US election and the upcoming French presidential elections similar?* *How is Atticus Finch's world similar to today's?*
Why is . . . important to . . .	*Why is 1930s art important to understanding the Great Depression?* *How was music important to the slave experience in the south?*
If . . . happened, how would . . . have changed or been different?	*If WWI had ended differently, would WWII have happened?* *If Henrietta Lacks' cells were not harvested, how would the medical research field have been different today?*
What are the underlying reasons for . . .?	*What are the underlying reasons for poverty?* *. . . the popularity of Romanticism in England and the United States?*

continued

TEACHER-GENERATED ESSENTIAL QUESTIONS *continued*	
Question Stems	**Sample Questions**
What are some problems of . . .?	*What are some of the problems with cloning?* *. . . environmental activism?* *. . . of converting religions in a non-secular state?*
How did/does . . . influence or impact . . .?	*How does language influence the way people see the world?* *How did the role of women in the Civil War influence the Suffragette Movement?*
Should . . .	*Should racial profiling be used in forensic cases?* *Should the music industry enforce tighter regulations in regards to sharing?*
How effective is . . .?	*How effective is Google Translate?* *How effective is the Electoral College?*
Which . . . is a better . . . (product/idea/law/ method/argument, etc.)?	*Which new product is better: the Apple iPhone or the Samsung Galaxy?* *Which is a better alternative energy method to pursue: wind or solar?*
Is there a possible solution to . . .?	*In a democracy, is there a possible solution to the influence money can have on politics?* *Is there a solution to America's gun violence?*
How could a . . . be designed to better/ improve . . .?	*How could the criminal justice system be improved?* *Healthcare research—student assessment/grades?*
Are we doing enough about . . . in our society?	*Are we doing enough to support students with mental illness in schools?* *Are we doing enough to support workers in obsolete industries?*
Should we/they . . .?	*Should we "celebrate" controversial holidays such as Columbus Day and Thanksgiving?* *Should minimum wage be visited yearly?*
What might occur if . . .?	*What might happen if our state legalized marijuana?* *What would happen if Yellowstone erupted?*

Ultimately, when thinking about questions for our students, we should keep this statement from McTighe and Wiggins in mind:

> The best essential questions are really alive. People ask, discuss, and debate them outside school. They arise naturally in discussion, and they open up thinking and possibilities—for novices and experts alike. They signal that inquisitiveness and open-mindedness are fundamental habits of mind and characteristic of lifelong learners. In a more practical sense, a question is alive in a subject if we really engage with it, if it seems genuine and relevant to us, and if it helps us gain a more systematic and deep understanding of what we are learning.

(2013, p. 8)

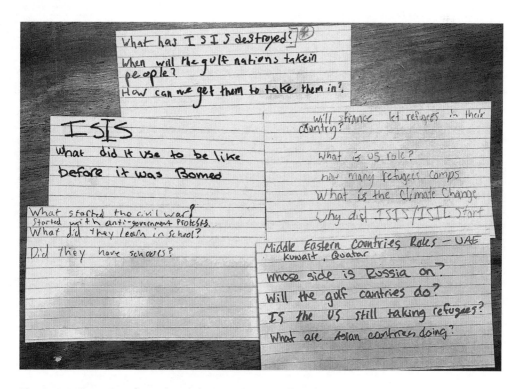

Figure 3.1 Questions formulated during a Syria study group

I would emphasize—don't get bogged down by what kinds of questions we are asking, but whether they spark interest, relevance, and desire for deeper learning in our students.

The poet, David Whyte, once wrote, "The marvelous thing about a good question is that it shapes our identity as much by the asking as it does by the answering." By guiding our students to come up with good questions, we not only guide their research, but we guide their minds and hearts into finding truth, making meaning of their worlds, and forming their identities. The power of questioning institutes greater strength in our students' critical thinking. It enhances their research, yes, but it also speaks to our secret curriculum of the heart.

 **TAKING A CLOSER LOOK**

Jeanie Phillips

Library

Jeanie Phillips, a high school librarian from Vermont, uses presearch with her students to build enough knowledge to help drive their essential and supporting questions in the classes she co-teaches with staff. Thoughtful about the importance of building a base to develop focus, Jeanie tells me, "Kids want to start taking their notes. They want to start answering their question before they even know what their question is."

To overcome this, Jeanie starts by having kids presearch until they are familiar with their topic AND still interested in it. Then they start to ask questions and brainswarm to finalize those questions. She tells them:

> For the next few days you are going to read lots. You should do enough reading—without taking notes—just reading—to be able to talk about this topic you're interested in for a full minute from your heart. And I say from the heart, because the best research projects happen when you're genuinely curious about something. By the end of your reading, I want you to ask yourself: Do I know enough to talk about my chosen subject for a full minute? Do I know enough to build good questions? Do I know enough to have a broad vocabulary that will build good searches later on?

> You won't be taking notes to answer your question, because you don't fully know what your question will be yet. That will come from the mind map you build after. While you read, use your presearch to broaden your vocabulary. You can jot down words and phrases that you haven't heard before or that stand out to you as expert vocabulary. Pay attention to what words you encounter. What vocabulary is showing up in your best sources? How can you use that vocabulary to get other really great sources? Use words from your sources, not just the words in your head. But this part is not about taking any notes. It's about being able to fully understand your topic.

When you have a topic that you love, write it in the center of the page and branch questions out from the topic. Some questions might be related to each other—clump those together or branch them off of each other. Then, we'll all present our questions to classmates, and everyone will provide feedback in the form of additional questions, opening closed questions, or asking related questions.

You'll use this feedback to revise your mind map—refine your questions and organize them. Put the question you are most interested in pursuing in the middle and surround it with supporting questions that might help you answer it.

MAP YOUR QUESTIONS

Background:

Albert Einstein famously said, "If I had an hour to solve a problem and my life depended on the solution, I would spend the first 55 minutes determining the proper question to ask." Asking questions is the first step to any information gathering process. A good research question has a Goldilocks quality to it: it's not too big but it's not too small, it's not too broad but it's not too narrow. Good research requires us to brainstorm questions that make us curious, do enough research to revise our questions, and hone in on a central question that is clear, focused, and open-ended.

Prompt:

Your task is to create and revise a mind map of questions, leading to one central research question.

PERFORMANCE TASK

Create a mind map of questions:

- Select topics and questions from your journal.
- Organize your topics and questions visually, grouping similar topics and questions.

Share your mind map, give and receive feedback:

- Share your questions and topics with your peers.
- Listen to feedback from your peers.
- Add new questions to your mind map.

Presearch your topic and revise your questions and map:

- Use your mind map to presearch your topic.
- Add and revise questions.
- Revise your mind map with your focus question in the center of the mind map and relevant sub-questions organized around the focus question.

CRITERIA FOR SUCCESS

	Getting Started	Developing	Proficient	Transfer
1.1.3 Develop and refine a range of questions to frame the search for new understanding.	I can ask questions, and recognize closed and open questions.	I can ask questions about a given focus. I can close open questions, and open closed questions.	I can ask, analyze, and revise questions given a focus.	I can use this skill in other settings, asking, analyzing, and revising questions for a focus of my own choosing.
Identify, manage, and assess new opportunities related to learning goals.	I can identify opportunities that pertain to my learning goals.	I can seek out information to help me make decisions and set goals and develop plans.	I can evaluate and pursue opportunities that pertain to my learning goals.	I can revise my goals and refine my plan based on time management, interpersonal interactions, personal reflection, and resources. I can create new opportunities by initiating, carefully selecting, and implementing appropriate approaches that pertain to my learning goals. I can reflect on the success of those approaches throughout the process.

#tldnr?

"Brainstorming and choosing a direction takes time and should start with . . . presearch: dedicated time for exploration."

"When students are given time to explore, their research becomes driven by curiosity, and we know that the best research takes place when we are genuinely curious."

"Presearch better prepares students to build research questions and search effectively with content-specific vocabulary."

"Coming up with good questions is the most important part of focusing our students' research experience."

"The essential question . . . is not a Google-able question . . . Supporting questions are your right-there look up questions."

"Scaffolding questions is a three step meta-cognitive process that includes generating, categorizing, prioritizing, and improving."

#tryonething

Ask students to come up with supporting questions.

Getting students to think metacognitively about their work will empower them as researchers. Instead of giving a list of topics they should include in their research or a list of questions, ask them to think backwards: what pieces of information will they need to know or what questions will they have to answer to draw conclusions and answer that bigger question? Have them use that list to drive their research.

4

So Much Out There
Helping Students Navigate the Vast Resource Landscape

It's 2014. Michael Brown, an 18-year-old teenager from Ferguson, Missouri, has been shot and killed by a police officer, and racial tensions are high. On Facebook and Twitter, an image of a young, black man, holding a gun to the camera with a wad of cash in his mouth starts circulating. News sources run the picture with titles like, "Ferguson's Michael Brown Pictured with a Gun—Flashing Gang Signs." Friends of mine repost the picture with heavily racist overtones, while accusing mainstream media of suppressing photo footage. Somehow the young man's death is justified in our collective consciousness because of this picture. Except for this: the picture isn't of Michael Brown. It's of another young man, Joda Cain, from Oregon, who was arrested for murder.

Ebola has incited fear in all of my students' hearts when they learn that a victim is being transported to a hospital in Boston, only an hour and a half away from us. "Mrs. Miller," one student says. "This is so scary. Because apparently ebola doesn't even kill you fully—you can come back from the dead. You thought *The Walking Dead* was fantasy? No way. We're moving in that direction right now." I laugh and reply, "I don't think you have to worry. There is no such thing as an ebola zombie." But another boy chimes in, "Yes there is! I saw it on the news—it's right here!" He pulls it up on his phone. "And here!" He shows me another article. And suddenly, yes. There are lots of ebola zombie articles online. But as we all know now, there is no such thing as an ebola zombie. Pictures from World War Z were doctored and one of the bodies filmed twitching was mistakenly declared dead ahead of time by a doctor who misread the severe symptoms.

In the thick of a heated and tumultuous presidential contest, ABC News posts an article about Executive Order 13738 that bans the Pledge of Allegiance from schools alongside a picture of President Obama signing the order at his desk. The commentary section is full of outraged people on both sides, slowly deconstructing into a mess of personal attacks and insults. A student shows this to me at school and says, "Can you believe this? I knew he was a dictator in disguise." As we examine other online sources, we discover news sites that attribute it to the AP. Most sites only reprint the first paragraph and don't include what comes later: other paragraphs about sock collecting, an ant-masturbatory dolphin, and a fake quote from the founder of Snopes. But here's what we know: this article wasn't posted on ABC News. It was posted on a site that simply *looks* like an ABC News site. The URL, www.abcnews.com.co, indicates that it is a knock off. And the author is a satirist. The AP never carried the news. The hyperlinks in the text take you to random places, the facts are skewed, and if you actually read the text of Executive Order 13738 on the federal government's website, you see that the Pledge of Allegiance isn't even mentioned. Yet, thousands of comments below the original article indicate that all of their readers were not able to recognize satire from news.

Finding and evaluating resources seems like an age-old problem that surely must have been solved by now, but instead it has become an epic issue that plagues and threatens excellent research. Assuming that our students have grown up using the Internet and know how to distinguish the credible from the false is dangerous for our communities. Our challenge must be showing students how to navigate through the vast amounts of information out there.

Let's Start in the Library

I have a basic belief that I am emphatic about: *all research should start in the library*. Several large studies of college students have shown that those who use the library for research experience greater academic success and retention. Sadly, though, most students will flounder and even fail in their research before they ask a librarian for assistance, while those who do, say that the librarian is the most helpful adult on campus when it comes to research (Head 2013; Kolowich 2011). But when we don't use the library in high school as part of the research process, we implicitly let students know that they can be successful without it, that Google is the singular route to research, and that libraries and the staff who work there are extraneous, ultimately setting them up for poor research practices when they reach post-secondary schooling.

When we start student research in the library, our students become comfortable with asking librarians for help, using books and periodicals, and accessing online library resources like databases. Even if the project does not entail using a physical book, it sets the tone: the library is always connected with research endeavors.

I am always stunned when I hear a teacher say that they don't need a library's services. Because here's the simple truth: using your library and librarian when taking on a research project *will always make your life easier.*

Collaborating with the librarian on research projects helps students indirectly, too, because it helps you as a teacher.

- The librarian is the only person in the building who sees students, academically, every year throughout the child's academic career. He or she knows every student and can provide you with invaluable information about the student's research skills.

- The librarian sees all content in all grades and can help ensure that your research expectations reinforce previously learned skills while pushing students to the next level.

- Librarians are experts at information curation and sorting and can help teachers with the monumental prep that goes into a research unit.

- Co-teaching with a librarian halves the student:teacher ratio, making the monumental task of conferencing with students about their processes much more manageable.

- Co-teaching always improves our practice. I have never worked with another teacher and not walked away a better teacher myself. Collaboration is essential for improving what we do. Two brains are always better than one!

- Librarians can dig in and save you a monumental amount of time by researching different project ideas like how to record podcasts, how to flip instruction, or how to make short documentaries.

In the library, of course, you can expect books. But your librarian can also direct you to databases, periodicals, primary sources, professional journals, movies, reference books, and more. He or she is an expert at finding resources —let them help make your and your students' jobs more efficient!

SAMPLE PLAN SHEET

Teacher: Laura Brusseau

Class: 9th grade

Dates: December 14–23

Essential question: How does the historic Supreme Court case you chose continue to affect our nation today?

Objectives: Understand how Supreme Court cases continue to affect us today; develop supporting research questions to guide inquiry (introduce); take notes that avoid plagiarism (master); synthesize multiple texts to develop a well-written thesis statement that can be supported (reinforce); purposefully integrate technology; write nonfiction across the curriculum.

Date	Time	Lesson
Dec 14	All classes, periods 1,2,3, and 4	Develop supporting questions and start reading resources (Angie) *Model difference between EQ and SQs *Show Supreme Court resources available
Dec 15	All classes	Reading and note-taking (Angie) *model note-taking strategies and revisit three non-negotiables
Dec 16	All classes	Reading and note-taking continued
Dec 17	All classes	Finish note-taking/ write draft of thesis statement (Laura)
Dec 18	All classes	Compiling information / website building (Angie, Laura, KarolBeth)
Dec 20	All classes	Compiling information / website building continued
Dec 21	All classes	Finish up . . .
Dec 23	All classes	Sharing websites/written reflection (Laura)

Working with your librarian: what to say!

When collaborating with your librarian...
...know what end product you have in mind and work backwards from there.
...sit together and discuss the content, literacy, and research objectives and determine how and when each of those could be met together.
...Ask questions like, "What are your ideas?" or "How would you...?" or "I was thinking...what do you think if...?"
...Use a planning sheet to document your plan together to eliminate any miscommunications and to lay out an agreed-upon shedule.
...do not present him or her with an entire lesson plan and ask to "plug them in."
...do not ask them to teach a lesson that jams every library skill into one class period.

When talking students with your librarian...
...inquire about other experiences they have had with your students.
...provide them with a class list so they can tailor their approach to the students.
...alert them to any IEPs, 504s, or behavioral issues you have encountered.
...ask them if there are any students who were successful using specific strategies.
...ask them what language and academic vocabulary was successfully used? What research skills did they cover in other classes?

When approaching your librarian about professional development...
...ask them if they have worked on any other projects similar to the one you are thinking of.
...ask them if there are other teachers in the building considering the same things.
...ask what their ideas are.
...ask them if they have resources.
...ask them which professional organizations the library subscribes to and whether or not there are journals available.

Figure 4.1 How to work with your librarian

Ready to plan with your librarian? Here is a sample sheet we use when teaming up. When planning, we start with the end. What content objectives do we want to meet? What research skills do we want to introduce/reinforce/master? What will the end product look like? Who will teach what? How long will each lesson take? After filling out this sheet, we share it with everyone involved so that everybody's plan books look the same and there is no confusion.

Becoming Search Savvy

Seventy-four percent of college freshmen report that they struggle with keywords and searches, and once they complete searches, nearly half of freshmen are overwhelmed by the amount of irrelevant information (Head 2013). In fact, "I can't find anything," is a frequent comment I hear when students embark on their research, whether they are using the Internet, a database, or an online book. I always ask, "What are you using for a search term?" and have discovered that our students type in the words that come first to their mind with no follow up, and only use the first few articles presented to them. When there is no helpful information on the first try, they get frustrated and stopped in their tracks.

Some teachers overcome this issue by providing all of the resources for their students, but there is great danger to this—finding and assessing resources is part of research. We need our students to wade through, filter, and critique the material that is out there and build the skills required to be fully fluent in the language of research.

Searching requires a certain savviness in language, and students who lack high level vocabulary struggle the most. But even those with limited vocabularies, can be successful in research if we give them the right tools.

- In conversation, provide students with search terms using your own prior knowledge. "Oh, when you're researching women's rights, you should look up Lucretia Mott." or "If you are studying disasters in the NASA program, start with the terms, 'Challenger' and 'Apollo 11.'" or "If you're interested in looking at juvenile diabetes, be sure to go to the Junior Diabetes Research Foundation." The goal is not to tell students what to do, but to use our knowledge to guide them into building their own.

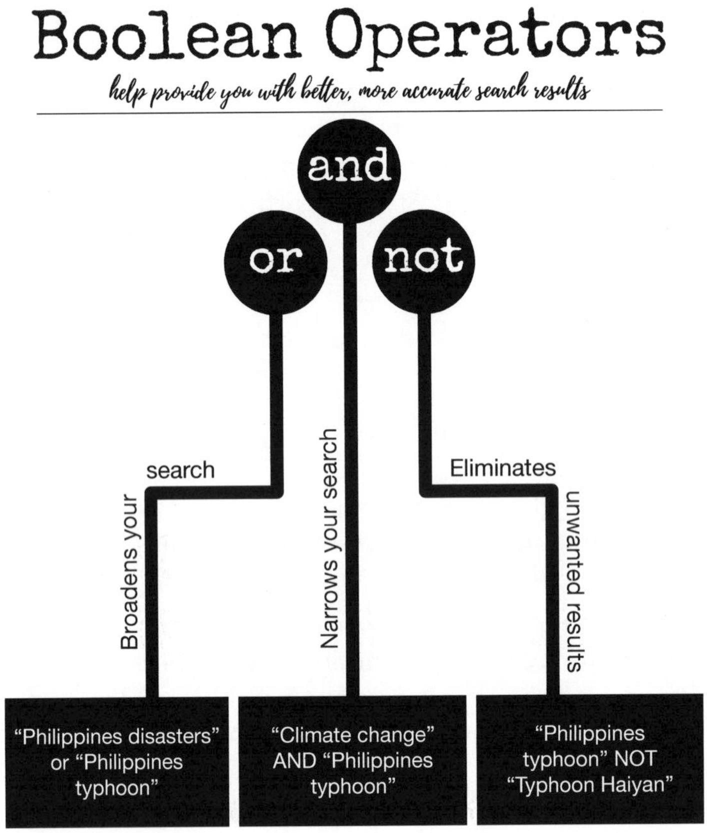

Boolean Operators

help provide you with better, more accurate search results

and

or **not**

Broadens your   search

Narrows your search

Eliminates   unwanted results

"Philippines disasters" or "Philippines typhoon"

"Climate change" AND "Philippines typhoon"

"Philippines typhoon" NOT "Typhoon Haiyan"

Figure 4.2 Boolean operators

- Teach students how to use Boolean phrases (see Figure 4.2).

- Encourage the use of an online thesaurus.

- Model, using your own search terms, how different results come up when you change the search.

- Show students how to use Wikipedia to come up with search terms.

- Talk about search terms regularly, so that students hear it as a normal part of the process that all learners have to grapple with. Ask them to reflect on what worked and what didn't work. Make it a metacognitve process.

Teaching Students to Use a Variety of Resources

I was working with a group of students on a research project and as I walked around the room, I noticed that several of them had Google searches open on their screens and were taking notes. They weren't actually on a website, they were jotting down information that showed up in the metadescription tags (the text underneath the URL). In this moment of horror, it suddenly dawned on me that many of our students struggle with the basic understanding of what makes a resource work for them and which ones they should be using.

Having Students Search Online Resources

The Internet is a labyrinth of resources that our students can get lost in, and there is a plethora of poor quality choices out there that they seem to gravitate towards. I once taught an entire lesson on credible sources during a philosophy project, and then when I sat with a student who was studying Voltaire, he told me his best resource was www.yolovoltaire.weebly.com. The challenge is always finding the balance between letting students seek out their own resources while not letting them get lost in a maze of poor choices.

Here are some strategies we can offer our students when they venture into Internetland on their own:

- **Read the URL**—Does it end with .gov? .com? .edu? .org? Note that this is just the beginning. There are some wonderful websites that end with .com and there are some terrible student papers shared on .edu websites. But being savvy enough to at least identify what kind of website they are looking at is important.

- **Alternative search engines**—Google isn't the only search engine! There are a variety of other search engines that make academic researching easier for students by culling out the important, reliable, credible sources. See "Alternative Search Engines" on p. 68 for a list of search engines that can assist students in accessing already-assessed information.

- **News sites**—Most major newspapers have entire sections focused on specific topics. So, students can search "New York Times Middle East" and find all of the *New York Times* articles on the Middle East. Housing, wars, climate change, women's issues, etc. are all common pages dedicated in the news.

ALTERNATIVE SEARCH ENGINES	
Search Engine	**Description**
Google Scholar	Google Scholar offers a place where students can search articles, books, court opinions that are published by professional organizations, universities, and academic websites.
iSeek	iSeek is an educational search engine that puts curated content from universities, governments, and established noncommercial providers at the fingertips of students and teachers.
Virtual Learning Resource Center	The VLRC pulls together thousands of sites selected by teachers and librarians with the mission to provide students at the secondary and post-secondary level with valid, current sources.
RefSeek	RefSeek's goal is to make researching easier for students by increasing the visibility of academic information. They have compiled over a billion documents.
SweetSearch	SweetSearch relies on 35,000 sites that have been curated by teachers, librarians, and research experts. It helps students focus their searches on more credible sites.

Using Databases

Many schools subscribe to online databases for their students' use. And many state libraries offer services like EBSCO or JSTOR to their public schools. Incorporating databases in academic studies can be frustrating, and often we don't ask student to use them because we're not sure how to use them ourselves. Many feel that because finding resources on Google is such an easy task, that databases are not necessary for research. But there are numerous benefits to utilizing databases as an academic resource, and if students understand how they can be used effectively, they find greater success.

WEBSITES TO SEND STUDENTS TO

ARTS	HEALTH
Arts Edge	Centers for Disease Control and Prevention
Google Art Project	Mayo Clinic
Grammy Museum	National Institute on Drug Abuse
Heilbrunn Timeline of Art History	National Alliance on Mental Illness
Louvre	National Institute of Mental Health
Metropolitan Museum of Art	National Organizations like: Juvenile
MOMA	Diabetes Research Organization
National Gallery of Art	National Institutes of Health
ProFotos	Psychology Today
Rolling Stone Magazine	World Health Organization

HISTORY	MATH
American Panorama	CIA World Factbook
CIA World Factbook	Get the Math
History Channel	Math Apprentice
Library of Congress	Mathematical Association of America
National Archives	New York Stock Exchange
Smithsonian Museums	Numberphile
Teachinghistory.org	Pew Research Center
US Holocaust Memorial Museum	Ted-Ed
Zinn Education Project	Vi Hart
	Wolfram-Alpha

SCIENCE	TECH AND COMPUTERS
American Chemical Society	Academic Earth
CK-12	HowStuffWorks
Discovery Channel	MIT World
NASA	PC Magazine
National Geographic	Popular Science
NOVA	Wired
Science Friday	Wolfram-Alpha
Scitable	Wonderopolis
Sparticl	

WORLD LANGUAGES/CULTURES	THE NEWS AND CURRENT EVENTS
BBC's Country Profiles	BBC
CIA World Factbook	New York Times
International Monetary Fund	PBS
Library of Congress' Portals to the World	Quartz
NationMaster	The Guardian
TIME for Kids	The Intercept
University of Richmond's Constitution Finder	Time Magazine
US Department of State	Wall Street Journal
	Washington Post

Here's what I tell kids:

> *Using databases is sometimes hard. Until you understand what they are and how they work. A database isn't a website. It's a filing system put together by a company. That company pulls together thousands of academic resources —journals, magazines, newspapers, encyclopedias—that I can't afford to purchase or house, and it categorizes them for us. We then pay a subscription and get to use their filing system.*
>
> *The largest benefit of using the databases is that all of the resources have been published by professionals. If they're showing up here, you know they're legit. They've all gone through an editorial process that most online resources don't go through. They've been checked for clarity and accuracy. They're updated frequently and their publication dates are always present, so you don't have to worry about getting bogged down in outdated information. And one of the coolest things? They provide your citation, so you don't have to worry about it being incorrectly formatted.*
>
> *One of our biggest mistakes when searching databases though, is that we try to search them like they're Google. And remember—this isn't a website. It's an online resource, so it doesn't necessarily act like a website. Make sure you use your Boolean phrases. If your search term is more than one word, put it in quotation marks and see what happens. If what you're looking for doesn't come up right away, try using alternative words. Try using the Advanced Search button.*
>
> *Sometimes we get a lot of returns on our searches and it's really time-consuming to read each and every source to see if it's going to help us. Instead, when you open the resource, there is often an abstract—a paragraph that gives an overview of the article itself. Read these to see if they are helpful. If not, get out of it and move to the next one.*
>
> *It takes a little practice, but you will find valuable sources here. It is where I want you to start. This is an academic research project, and these databases will consistently provide you with academic research.*

When assigning a new research project, tell your students that you expect them to use academic resources. Work with your librarian and see which databases are available and have him or her co-teach a lesson with you on how to access and easily use the databases for their projects.

Books

Books *are* still a thing, after all! It seems silly to say this, but my students are always surprised by how useful books are. To get them to readily and habitually use books, though, we have to seek titles out and put them directly into students' hands. Even if I grab a stack of books and set them down on a table near students, they still will not gravitate towards them. However, every time I sit next to a student while he or she is reading resources, hand them an open book, and say, "Hey, I just came across this chapter and thought you might be interested. It's about your topic," they always use the book. From there, they will often tell other classmates if they see something that will help their projects, and they also become repeat visitors to the library, asking for books for research. It's not enough to tell students to use books—we have to show them the value of using them.

Assessing Resources

With the wealth of resources available, the problem for our students isn't finding resources anymore; it's deciding which ones are best to use in which circumstances. It's dangerous to assume that because our students are growing up with search engines in their back pockets they fully understand how to define credibility. And with the onslaught of false information available, this skill has become more pressing than ever. We must guide students through the process of assessing what they read.

To do that, I like to use California State University's CRAAP Test. It asks students to examine Currency, Relevancy, Authority, Accuracy, and Purpose.

Let's break that down. Here is what I tell students:

Currency

Currency really depends on the topic. If you are studying Lincoln's assassination, an older document is going to be acceptable. But if you are delving into cancer research, you need to make sure that they have the most recent information available. Science, medicine, computers, careers, technology, current events, world cultures—you want that to be written as recently as possible. It is the responsible thing to do. History, literature, biographies—those are a little more flexible because they don't change with ongoing research for the most part. Database documents will always have dated entries, but sometimes websites do not. Scroll to the bottoms of articles and read the dates. Currency is critical to credibility.

Relevancy

When you're thinking about relevancy, of course you have to think about topical relevancy—does this really have to do with my topic? But we also have to think about intended audience. Is this document written for you? Is it written for a younger audience? Is the text too difficult? Is the information important enough to include? Do you need to read the whole text or just a section of it? Irrelevant information can bog your process down.

Authority

It is important to assess the credibility of the person or organization who is writing this piece. Who is the author? Do they have credentials? Is this information put out by a professional organization? Has the information been tested or reviewed? Look and see if there is an About Us section on the website and read it carefully. Determine: is this author an expert in his or her field? When you cite work that does not hold authority, you lose your own authority in your research. Don't put yourself in a position where your audience dismisses you because you have undermined your own academic work

Accuracy

This part is harder to test, but essential to all research. A friend once told me that you are not entitled to your opinion when you do research—you are only entitled to hold positions that you can support by facts. I had to think hard about that, but ultimately, I think I believe the same thing. We can disagree with one another on any topic, but our arguments must be grounded in truth. You want to make sure that the work you are citing is accurate and reliable. If there is no consistent veracity to your work, you lose credibility.

There are ways to check for truth when reading. Question your sources. If you read something that seems controversial, look and see if it is written elsewhere on other sites that are credible and truthful. Check sites like Snopes or Politifact. You have to be a fact checker. This is called reading laterally. When we read across sources, we verify facts. If we only read vertically— meaning reading straight through a source without questioning or verifying it, we are less likely to uncover any misperceptions. This is dangerous in the research world. Untruths can spread like wildfire on the Internet.

There are people who make money publishing false information, and so they keep producing it without any concern of what that does to our society. Be sure you are not spreading untruths. Ensuring that your research relies on truthful, accurate information is a responsibility you must take seriously.

Purpose

The news is a tricky place to look online these days. In the past, there were news articles and there were editorials. The purpose of articles is to inform. The purpose of editorials is to convince. But now media companies blur the lines, fluidly moving between reporting and giving opinion. How do you know when this is happening? The headline is the best place to start. If the headline feels more like an opinion statement than an observation, it probably has bias. If you go to news sites like The Washington Post, the New York Times, the Wall Street Journal, the Chicago Tribune, your local newspaper, etc. you'll notice that they usually have articles labeled as "World News" or "Local News" or "Opinion." Be aware of tone, language used, and whether or not the author is writing from an objective standpoint—one that reports the events—or from a subjective standpoint—one that comments on the events.

It's okay to use opinion pieces to guide your research—you may find people who support their arguments with verifiable facts. You may encounter authors who challenge your thinking. The danger is when you don't know that this is what they are trying to do. Do not confuse news with commentary.

When reading any piece, ask yourself—why is this out there? Why did the author write this? In a recent Stanford study, they found out that kids like you have a hard time determining whether an online source is an article or an advertisement, because advertisement companies are getting really savvy at making their stuff appear legit. Look for that—is somebody trying to sell you something? Are they trying to convince you of something? Again, it's okay to use pieces like this, but only if you are knowingly looking for a piece that offers an opinion. Do not cite opinion as fact. What we believe and feel is not the same as facts.

Knowing your author or organization's purpose will help you assess what the piece is for and how you will use it. Just don't get duped into using something out of context.

We all tell students to use reliable sources. I know we do. But as the Internet becomes a more complicated interweb of ideas and publications, our students struggle with what "reliable" means. Explicit conversations like this help them unpack what we mean and give them the skills to assess credibility. Online, the University of California has a great resource that can be printed and shared with our students to go along with this discussion.

But What about Wikipedia?

Wikipedia is a touchy subject. Many teachers see the value in the sixth most often-visited website in the world, and since its inception, vandalism and fraudulent entries have dropped to only a 7% occurrence rate (Malone-Kircher 2016). Certainly, most of us use it in our day-to-day lives. But many university professors will not accept the crowd-sourced site as legitimate for academic research. So the conundrum always arises: do we let kids use Wikipedia or not?

I think it's important to look what Wikipedia says about itself to draw final conclusions. On its "Citing Wikipedia" page, they make the following statement:

> We advise special caution when using Wikipedia as a source for research projects. Normal academic usage of Wikipedia and other encyclopedias is for getting the general facts of a problem and to gather keywords, references and bibliographical pointers, but not as a source in itself. Remember that Wikipedia is a wiki, which means that anyone in the world can edit an article, deleting accurate information or adding false information, which the reader may not recognize.
>
> (Wikipedia: Citing Wikipedia)

And on its "Academic Use" page, this statement is made:

> Citation of Wikipedia in research papers may be considered unacceptable, because Wikipedia is not considered a credible or authoritative source ... Remember that any encyclopedia is a starting point for research, not an ending point.
>
> (Wikipedia: Academic Use)

All encyclopedias are considered tertiary sources—and good research practices should rely more on primary and secondary sources. No research project should solely rely on encyclopedias.

So does that mean our students shouldn't use Wikipedia?

Of course our students should use Wikipedia! We just need to show them responsible ways the site can be used within academic research.

Search Terms
It is difficult to execute an efficient, productive search if a student doesn't have any background knowledge. When undertaking new topics, Wikipedia

gives students precise, subject-specific search terms. Have students look for important places and places and pay attention to subheadings. These terms can be used for students to find valuable information in academic resources.

General Knowledge
Wikipedia is a great stop in for finding common knowledge like dates, places, names, etc.

Other Sources
At the end of each Wikipedia article is a list of other sources. Have students use that as a launching pad to more reliable primary and secondary sources.

Open Source Pictures
If pulling together a final presentation, Wikipedia's pictures are in the public domain, meaning students can use them without worry about licensure. When a user clicks on the picture, everything needed to cite a picture—the artist, the title, the date, and the subject—is all made available.

Managing Resources

I've lined up all of this work with students and felt successful—they have great topics, they're reading great resources, they're starting to take notes. And then I sit with one and ask where she got a certain piece of information that she's having a hard time understanding and she says she's not sure. She can't remember. Or I'll have a student tell me something important he read, but he can't remember where he read it and he spends 15 minutes going through his search history. And suddenly I feel like the entire research project is imploding and unraveling. I torment myself with thoughts like *If I had only done x . . . If I hadn't done y . . . Does any of this even matter anymore?* I find myself taking a deep breath of frustration.

Does any of this sound familiar? It's the management-oriented things like this that drive us nuts when teaching research.

Helping students develop an efficient management system early in the process eliminates these little moments that blindside us. Before students start collecting their resources, let them know:

> *It's important to keep track of all of your resources. All too often, we close out of a website by accident or can't find a helpful article from a database we were reading yesterday. Sometimes we read things and then move on to something else, and later realize that we want to go back to it, but can't*

eRESOURCES

MANAGEMENT TOOLS

Tool	How It Works	Other Information
Evernote	Evernote acts like a bookshelf that has three ring binders on it. Users build and name notebooks, download a "pin" tool to their task bar, and then pin websites as they find them. The websites are saved to their virtual notebook, so there is a collection of everything in one place.	The free version of Evernote (www.evernote.com) is adequate for students. This is my favorite management system, because it allows you to modify the text that is saved in the notebook—users can delete everything irrelevant on a website and keep what they want; they can bold or underline important information; they can put in check boxes next to facts they want to include later. I could not have written this book without Evernote—I use it every day, and while some kids resist learning a new system like this, many incorporate it into all of their academics.
Google Docs	A simple Google Doc is a great place for students to keep copied and pasted hyperlinks. If the user builds a new folder for his research project, starts a new document, and labels it "Resources," it is easy to access and find.	Many students prefer using Google Docs because it is a system that they are already familiar with. Students who end up taking notes in a Google Doc like having the resource right there at the top of the page to keep track of where the notes came from.
EasyBibEDU	Teachers apply for a free school code and then their students have access to developing a Works Cited as they collect sources, note-taking, outlining; website assessing (using the CRAAP test), etc. in MLA, APA, Chicago, and any other citation guide you might want to use.	EasyBib is the greatest invention since the sticky note. Most of our students are aware of how to build a Works Cited, but there is so much more available in the EDU version. EasyBib offers online webinars that walk you through their products. While middle school platforms are ad-free, the high school version does have minimal ads.
Noodle Tools	Noodle Tools offers many of the same services as EasyBib, only with a cleaner look.	NoodleTools is a paid-subscription service, so no ads will appear in any of the services it offers. For the services it offers, it is extremely affordable. It is compatible with Google Docs and provides access to APA and other citation guides (not allowed under EasyBib). It also has students manually enter information into their citation tool, resulting in more accurate WorksCiteds.

remember where it is. Right? I know I've had all of these things happen during the research process, and it's extremely frustrating!

So what I'm going to show you are some tools to keep track of your resources. It doesn't matter which tool you use or how you use it—what matters is that you can go into your system and put your hands on what you need when you need it in a timely manner. What matters is that you will be able to find the title, the author, the date you found this, and where it is located easily. It's a little bit of extra work in the beginning, yes, but it makes everything so less frustrating for you and will save you immense amounts of wasted time in the end.

Primary Sources

Primary sources are the ultimate research source—they provide incredible insight. Listening to Martin Luther King's speech is more telling of what happened that day than reading about it on a tertiary website. Reading excerpts of Marie Curie's journals is better than reading about her on a biography encyclopedia. Pictures of Nazi concentration camps are more rich than any textbook description.

When I co-taught the Revolutionary War with my social studies teacher, we would ask the students the question, *Should John Adams have represented the British soldiers in court after the Boston Massacre?* Students would read the *Boston Gazette*'s news article about the events that day, other eyewitness accounts, Paul Revere's engraving, and Adams' reflections, and then try to decide what happened at the massacre and whether Adams should have taken those steps as a lawyer.

Primary documents are resources that allow students to better ask their own questions and draw their own conclusions, whereas secondary and tertiary resources often pre-emptively draw conclusions for them. The Library of Congress calls primary documents the "raw materials of history." Because of primary documents, we know about the moon landing, Anne Frank, Shackleton's trip to Antarctica, and the powerful delivery of Obama's 2004 DNC keynote address. They are the visual, written, and oral histories of humanity.

But finding ways to use primary documents in authentic, meaningful ways can be tricky. The language is often difficult, the context can be hard to pull out, or we just have a difficult time finding the "right" ones. Here are some ideas for how to overcome the primary source obstacles and have students use them as research resources:

- Use the Library of Congress' primary source evaluation tool
(www.loc.gov/teachers/primary-source-analysis-tool/) to jumpstart
questioning. Give students a source (or pictures) to closely examine
at the beginning during their presearch stage. Ask them to observe:
What do you see/hear/read? What do you notice? Then ask them to reflect:
*What do you think is happening? What do you think the purpose was? Who
do you think the audience was?* And then move them to questioning,
asking them to use investigative questions that start with words like,
Who? What? Where? When? How? Why? From this activity, students
can build a base of questions that will drive their research.

Figure 4.3 Library of Congress primary document used to start the question process

We do this in US History II when we show students a picture of a car that is
on a dirt road. We ask them first to observe, and they notice that it is a black
and white picture; that the driver appears to be shot; there may be another
passenger in the vehicle; the car is an old one; there are large holes in the car—
bigger than bullet holes; it's an intersection; dirt road; tires are shot out from
the car. We then ask them to reflect and they start saying things like, "I think
there was some kind of crime happening. Maybe the mob was involved." "It
looks like Bonnie and Clyde." "I think they were running from the police and
the police took this picture." Next, we tell them that this picture was taken on
December 7, 1941 in Pearl Harbor and four people are dead in that car. What
questions do they have? Surprised by the context of the picture, the students
easily move into asking questions like, *How many civilians were killed that day?*

What was the effect on the general population, not just the military? Were the people who lived there given any notice? Were they able to escape? Did the Japanese bomb just the ships, or did they bomb inland, too?

This activity naturally starts them thinking about and asking questions that can help spark their final essential question.

- Use primary sources to have students better understand their research. When students listen to speeches, read journals, and closely examine maps, they will better understand the story behind their research.

One year I worked with a student who was wondering if technology had been more advanced, would any of da Vinci's inventions been reliable? He was really struggling to find resources that allowed him to draw his own conclusions. For the most part, he was only finding biographies on da Vinci. "Have you looked at da Vinci's notebooks?" I asked him. He hadn't. We found an online version of all of da Vinci's notebooks, and the student lost himself to flipping through the pages. He suddenly could *see* what da Vinci was imagining. And he was able to say—No. DaVinci's drawings would not have been successful because they defied physics. He narrowed in on his flight machine and compared it to the Wright Brothers' successful flight at Kitty Hawk, outlining the differences in structures.

- Use pictures so students can write better papers. Writing research does not need to be the equivalent to writing boring. We want students' words to spark interest for their audience. When students can create imagery in their writing, this takes place.

When I work with an English teacher on a Victorian England research paper, we ask students to spend some time really closely looking at pictures of children in factories, orphanages, women's clothing, houses, city streets, family life, etc. We have discovered that when they can visualize their topic, they write more descriptive, interesting papers. We show them research work from authors like Jim Murphy, James Swanson, and Rosalyn Schanzer to emphasize how primary documents augmented and improved the writing.

Having students listen to speeches can allow them to include the speaker's charisma and effectiveness in their writing. When students read newspaper articles and political cartoons they can attest to bias. Primary sources broaden the spectrum in which they see and write about their topic.

Research will only ever be as good as the resources used. In a culture full of rhetorical strife and disagreement, it is critical that we embed the lessons of seeking truthful and credible information into our daily practices. It is the skill that our students need in order to navigate messy political arenas, mixed media messages, and social media barrages. Every moment invested in teaching our students how to assess and dig into credible information is a moment invested in the future of decency and democracy.

GREAT PLACES TO FIND PRIMARY SOURCES	
Authentic History Center	An easy-to-search site that documents American history through pop culture, from the 1600s to present day.
Docs Teach	A rich online tool from the National Archives that not only gives a searchable database of primary sources, but also provides tools for teachers to use in the classroom.
Fordham University's Internet History Sourcebooks Project	This is a collection of public domain and copy-permitted historical texts. It is not as current as some of the better-maintained sites, but still has valuable offerings.
Library of Congress	The largest, most varied source of primary documents available, with recent focus on how to use in the classroom.
Life Photo Archives	Partnered up with Google, this archive offers millions of photographs from the 1750s to today.
Smithsonian Museum	A searchable collection of all of the Smithsonian museums that delves into American History.
Yale Law School Avalon Project	This site focuses on documents in law, history, and diplomacy from ancient times to the twenty-first century.
Other places to look: art museums; historical societies; professional membership organizations.	

TAKING A CLOSER LOOK

Brianna Crowley

English

Brianna Crowley, a National Board Certified high school English teacher in Hershey, Pennsylvania, found herself experimenting every year with new ways to help students learn relevant research skills. But no matter which tactic she took, she found there was always a deep disconnect between how students searched during research-focused class time and when searching for projects in other classes. In other words, the research skills learned in English class weren't being transferred, and students weren't internalizing these lessons as inherently useful.

Brianna realized that her research lessons and practice assignments needed to incorporate more reflection and metacognition, less rote practice with research skills, and more application of skills. She decided to limit the amount of direct instruction and plan more time for student-driven exploration paired with explicit reflection questions. Through this, her Process Log resource was born.

After Brianna and her school librarian worked together to introduce strategies like using Boolean operators and synonyms for creating strong search queries, they introduce the Process Log to the students, saying:

> Today you will be applying all of the lessons we've discussed about searching strategies, tools, and platforms. To review, who can briefly summarize the Boolean operators we learned and how they help us create a strong search query? . . . To review, what is the difference between search strategy and a search tool? . . . What are some search tools Google offers that can help narrow or broaden your search? . . . What are the advantages of using a database rather than an Internet search engine?

> OK, now that we have that review fresh in our head, let's take a look at the process log you will be filling out. You are encouraged to have any notes or previous materials out to help you in this search. The goal of this exercise it to see which strategies and tools actually work for you and see the direct correlation between using them and finding reliable and helpful resources more quickly. Remember, our goal is not to scroll aimlessly through a bunch of Google pages hoping a great resource appears. Our goal is to do a few seconds of thinking at the start of the search in order to save a whole lot of time scrolling after the search.

> After you each complete this process log, you will receive feedback from Mrs. Crowley and you may be asked to share your results in small groups so that you can learn from your peers as well.

> Please note that the front page asks you to complete a search for a text-based resource while the second page asks you to find multi-media resources. You should also note on the second page that you are asked to provide reasoning for why you chose a search engine or database.

> Any questions about this assignment and the goals for completing it?

Name _____ Class/Period _____ Date _____

RESEARCH PROCESS LOG:
TEXT-BASED RESOURCE USING A SEARCH ENGINE

Search Terms and Key Words

List all the **search terms** you will use to find a resource from the Internet.
If applicable, show the **Boolean operators**, **phrase searching strategies**, and
word combinations you will/did try.

_____

_____

_____

Search Engine: What did you use? _____

Within that, what **TOOLS** did you use to narrow, widen, or refine your search?
List the TOOLS below and offer a brief explanation of their effect on your
search.

Tool: *Explanation* _____

_____

Tool: *Explanation* _____

_____

Tool: *Explanation* _____

_____

Reflection

How did your initial searches strategies work? How many results did you
receive? What adjustments did you make in order to find useful resources?
Please include answers to all of these questions in paragraph form below.

_____

_____

_____

_____

_____

_____

_____

Name _____ Class/Period _____ Date _____

RESEARCH PROCESS LOG:
MULTI-MEDIA RESOURCE USING DATABASE OR SEARCH ENGINE

Search Terms and Key Words

List all the **search terms** you will use to find a multi-media resource from the Internet. If applicable, show the **Boolean operators**, **phrase searching strategies**, and **word combinations** you will/did try.

_____

_____

_____

Database or Internet?

Will you do this search with a database or Internet or both? First identify database or Internet by circling, and then explain what **TOOLS** you used to narrow, widen, or refine your search. List these TOOLS below and offer a brief explanation of their effect on your search.

Search 1 DATABASE | INTERNET

Tools used: _____

_____

Results _____

_____

Search 2 DATABASE | INTERNET

Tools used: _____

_____

Results _____

_____

Reflection

How did your initial searches strategies work? What adjustments did you make in order to find useful resources? What did you learn about searching for multi-media vs. text? Answer in paragraph form below.

_____

_____

_____

#tldnr?

"Assuming that our students have grown up using the Internet and know how to distinguish the credible from the false is dangerous for our communities."

"All research should start in the library."

"74% of college freshmen report that they struggle with keywords and searches, and once they complete searches, nearly half of freshmen are overwhelmed by the amount of irrelevant information."

"Ask students to examine Currency, Relevancy, Authority, Accuracy, and Purpose when assessing resources."

"Helping students develop an efficient management system early in the process eliminates [the] little moments that blindside us."

"Primary sources are the ultimate research source—they provide incredible insight."

#tryonething

Plan your next research unit with your librarian.

Remember, when we use the library, we implicitly let our students know: this is an important place for academic research. Ask your librarian to help co-teach lessons, gather resources, grade Works Citeds. Ask her what s/he knows about the students' research backgrounds. Ask them for their ideas. Keep them on board as part of the entire research process, not just the launching pad.

5

Take Note

Introducing Strategies that
Improve Student Learning and Help
Them Avoid Plagiarism

As I sat next to Cameron, a ninth grade writer, to read his research paper draft, I could tell immediately that entire chunks of his writing had been pulled directly from somebody else's writing. The vocabulary, syntax, and sentence structure drastically changed for sentences at a time. Whenever I catch somebody plagiarizing, I am overwhelmed by a stomachful of dread. It is such an uncomfortable conversation to have.

"Cameron," I gently started. "It looks as though these may not be your words. As though you copy and pasted sections from somebody else's writing." Cameron looked at me with genuine concern and shook his head. "No, Mrs. Miller, you taught us not to do that."

"Then how can you explain this? Because it looks like copying and pasting," I pushed back a little.

> I did not copy and paste. I printed off my resources, highlighted the parts I liked and then hand wrote them onto a notecard and *then* typed them into my paper. I *did not* copy and paste them. That would be plagiarizing.

This moment stopped me in my teaching tracks. This was an otherwise capable student who took pride in his work and generally behaved with integrity. How did he completely miss the meaning of plagiarizing? His literal understanding of copying and pasting interfered with his recognition of who owns ideas and words.

From this point on, when teaching about note-taking, I no longer stopped at "copy and paste" instructions—instead, I talk about words and ideas. I begin by telling students that the writing they read is written by published writers who have advanced degrees in their subject area. That those writers have worked hard to become experts in their field. I ask them if they've ever worked on a group project and had somebody get a good grade because of their work—most kids nod at this. And I tell that that feeling of being robbed of the deserved credit is what plagiarism is. That our words and our ideas belong to us—they make up our belief systems and our intellect. And we have no right to take that away from any writer. So we have to make sure, when doing research, that we respect the rights of the experts we rely on. And I tell them that the first step to avoiding this invasion of intellectualism is to take good notes.

The P Word

I need to be honest: I hate note-taking. I am an impulsive, impatient writer who wants to just read through material and then throw ideas down on paper. And when I first started teaching, I thought note-taking and outlining were synonymous with sucking the creative liquid out of anybody's pen. Teaching note-taking is difficult, and requiring it is time-consuming. And as I watch other teachers teach research, I can tell I am not the only one who has grappled with these ideas. My experience has shown me that note-taking is truly the most important part of compiling research, yet it is the most oft-skipped step. Sometimes students are told to "take notes," but rarely are they shown how to do that, nor are those notes ever given feedback. What I have discovered over the years though, is that the time invested in teaching notes is well worth any hesitation we may have. They improve how we teach the writing process (see Chapter 6), but they also address something we always worry about when teaching research: plagiarism.

Most students do not actually mean to plagiarize. "I read words and cannot imagine another possible way to say it," one student told me. Another confided, "I just write down what the author said and figure I'll change it later, but then I forget which are my words and which are somebody else's." Unconscious plagiarism occurs when our students do not monitor their sources closely (Harris 2001) and they, like me, are often too impatient to train themselves to be thorough monitors. They want to write down what they see and move on. But if we help students take careful notes, we help them avoid this unconscious plagiarism. Good note-taking strategies are the key to avoiding unintentional plagiarism.

> *Remember, you are reading the writing of somebody who makes a living writing,* I tell kids. *Their words are going to be good—they've worked hard at constructing their pieces. But you're not looking for the right words right now, you're looking for the right ideas to back up what you want to say. When I read words and have to take notes, it's like trying to sing another song while a catchy tune is on the radio. They're the only construction of language I can see—I can't imagine another way to say it. So here's a trick: read a paragraph and then get your eyes away from it—it's like turning off the radio. Close your computer or book and think about what you just read. What were the most important parts? Make a list of what you just learned. Now you're going to be using your own words, not somebody else's. It'll help stop you from singing the song that's on the radio.*

The Non-negotiables

When explicitly teaching note-taking I have four non-negotiables:

1. Notes must be handwritten.
2. Notes must be in your own words.
3. Notes must be written in phrases, not complete sentences.
4. Notes need to be tracked back to each source.

Notes Must Be Handwritten

What I tell students:

> *Your brain works in fascinating ways. Strangely, the part that works when you write things down is different than the part that works when you type something. It's much easier for our brains to type information verbatim without us having to think about what we're doing, whereas, when we handwrite information we have to process and conceptualize it a little differently. What this means for you is that handwriting your notes improves your learning. The process of reading, thinking about what you are going to write, and then physically writing activates the memory parts of your brain.*

Notes Must Be in Your Own Words

What I tell students:

> *The process of getting from the information you are reading to what you have to write involves a few steps. First, you have to read it and understand it. Then you have to take notes on it. After you organize those notes, you write about it. So, what this means is your notes become your outline, which becomes your writing. If your notes are in your own words, you won't unintentionally plagiarize in the end. You'll have original work to pull from. If you're stuck, and you're not sure how to put something in your own words, turn to a friend and just tell them what you've been reading about. Give me a shout and we can talk through it. Sometimes just verbally walking through some information helps you write originally.*

Notes Must Be in Phrases, Not Complete Sentences

What I tell students:

> *This part of the note-taking process stems from me being a writing teacher. As I've said before, your notes become your outline and your outline becomes your writing. If your notes are already in complete sentences, then your outline will become a block of sentences and your paper will become a bunch of sentences strung together, rather than a piece of writing that includes your information. Writing sentences in isolation of one another will result in a choppy, elementary-like product. It removes flow, sophistication, wordplay, and a variety of sentence structures from your writing. When we get to the writing part, I'll expand more on this and help you with it, but for now, know that this is where we are going and to make that step a better piece for you, these notes should be in short phrases.*

Notes Need to Be Tracked Back to Each Source

What I tell students:

> *There is nothing worse in the research process than going to cite a fact and not knowing where it came from. This happens all the time to the best of us. We write something down and forget to keep track of where it came from, and then have to rifle through all of our sources looking for it. It's frustrating and a waste of time. How you keep track of sources is up to you—here are some ways that I've seen it done:*
>
> - *Take notes on different colored sticky notes. Maybe each topic has its own color. Maybe each source has its own color.*

- *Number each source and put that number next to the note (and on the source so you remember!)*
- *Color code each source and have every note from your first source written in red and every note from your second source written in blue, etc.*
- *Write all your notes from one source on one piece of paper.*

There are lots of different ways to keep track—which way you do it isn't important; what is important is that you can go back and say these notes came from these resources.

What Are They Taking Notes On?

I was working with a religion teacher who had asked students to research a major religion in the world and, integrating current events, answer the essential question: How does this religion play a role in today's world? When I sat down to conference with a student, she showed me her work—she had two entire pages of notes on the history of Chanukah. The source she was using was good, the information was accurate and interesting, and the notes were taken well, but the relevancy of the material didn't match up with the project itself.

This happens a lot—when looking at how philosophers impact the US Constitution, students will take notes about the philosophers' parents' names. When looking at how Shakespeare impacted the English language, they will include information about where he was born. On the other hand, when studying anxiety, they will leave out possible treatments. Overwhelmed by the amount of information at their fingertips, they either take notes on everything or not enough. How do we help them determine what is valuable information to include?

It goes back to those questions. When students have created supporting questions, they have begun to structure their purpose for reading. Here's what I tell them:

There is a lot of information out there on your topics, but remember, you are writing a paper, not a book. So that means you have to be a little more discriminating about what information you are going to include. Even if the information is interesting, it may not be important to your task at hand. So first, let's look at that essential question. That is what you are going to try to answer in the end. Don't look for the answer now. The answer to that is your own conclusion. But everything you write down should be helping build that answer—and that's where your supporting questions come in.

Before reading your sources, reread your supporting questions. Those are going to help set your purpose for reading. Now, of course, you might bump into some other information that you hadn't thought you would need. Include that, yes! But use those supporting questions as a framework for your purpose.

Now, here's a trick somebody taught me in grad school when reading through these longer sources. Look at the structure of the writing. Use the subheadings to determine if you need to read through a section. And then, as you do read through, pay attention to those topic sentences. Read the topic sentence of a paragraph. Is it biographical information that isn't necessary? Skip ahead. Is it a sentence that starts to focus on something you think will be pertinent? Slow down. When reading for research, we need to prioritize—it's impossible to read everything, and it's not wise to take notes on irrelevant information— but at the same time, you want to make sure that you are not missing important information. So keep your supporting questions out at all times. Let them drive your purpose.

How Are They Taking Notes?

"Be sure to take notes," I say, and the students nod and get to looking busy. Sound familiar? It took me a long time to realize that what I think "taking notes" means may not be what others think it means. It also took me a long time to realize that while there are some non-negotiables in taking notes, how we actually do it needs to work for our individual brains. It is important to show students a variety of different methods of note-taking strategies and let them determine which techniques will best help them access and remember the information.

Notecards
Tried and true, the notecard is the mainstay of note-taking. No matter how many different methods I show students, there are always some that stay with this. And while it seems as though everybody was once taught the notecard method at one time or another, I taught my husband when he was in college, so not everybody knows how to take notes on notecards. *Put one fact on each notecard* I tell students. *This will allow you greater flexibility when arranging your notes for organizational, pre-writing purposes*

Cornell Notes
Of course, Cornell notes are another good standby. The two-column process allows students to identify key points in the first column and then expand on

those in the second column. The nice thing about Cornell notes is that they automatically lend themselves to the metacognitive practices discussed later in this chapter that include questioning and reflection.

Big Paper Flow-based Notes

There is something about big paper and colored pens or thin-tipped markers that appeals to the oldest student we teach. Many students like using all red markers for one source and all blue markers for another. They spread all of their information out onto a large piece of blank paper and draw arrows and circles to create subcategories or to develop a flow of ideas. Students who take notes this way then rewrite them when organizing them, but the process of being able to spread it out onto one sheet of paper helps them see the larger picture.

Sticky Notes

I am a huge fan of sticky note notes! When taking notes on sticky notes, students can color code their topics—so maybe all the facts about their first subtopic are on the pink notes. And all the facts about their second subtopic are on the yellow ones. My favorite way to use sticky notes, though, is to color code them by source—so all of the pink ones represent the first resource and all the yellow ones represent the second. This means students don't have to remember which source each fact came from—they just have to remember which source goes with which color. When stepping into the organizational phase, the sticky notes are easily organized and moved around.

Metacognitive Notes

As teachers we know why we want students to take notes—we want them to have the information they need to draw conclusions. But often, that gets lost in translation for students and they see it as a step they have to do because the teacher wants them to. They do not always value or understand the process.

This is where metacognition (thinking about one's thinking) comes into play. We want students to learn from the material they are reading and write it in ways that help them think beyond the facts. We want them to make connections and see similarities and contradictions within their worlds. Learning when to paraphrase, when to quote, and when to reflect provides them the opportunity to take those leaps.

Here's what I tell kids when teaching metacognitive strategies:

When you are reading text, you want to ask yourself two questions: 1. Is this important to my study? And 2. If it is, why? The answer to that second question is what helps you determine what kind of note to write down. Is it a fact that helps support your argument or explain your topic? Then you want to write it down so you can paraphrase and summarize in your final piece. When you paraphrase, you are rewriting the author's message in your own words. You are getting the entire message to your reader. Remember, this is hard to do when you are staring at the word choice and sentence structure of the author. Read it and get it away from your eyes. Jot down the important things. When you summarize, you are doing something a little different—you are condensing the material; you are only taking the key points down—the main ideas. Again, get the writer's words away from you and make a list of those main ideas. Have you ever seen the movie Ten Things I Hate About You? *It's an old 90s romantic comedy that made Heath Ledger a star about a younger sister who isn't allowed to date until her older, more abrasive, sister has a boyfriend. So the younger sister starts trying to set her uncharming sister up. What I just told you was a summary of the story. But the movie itself? It's a giant, cinematical paraphrase—it's the same story as* The Taming of the Shrew *by Shakespeare—just told in a new way. When you are taking notes, you have to decide—is this information worth retelling? Or is it better to just summarize?*

Sometimes, an author says something that is worth quoting. I'll sometimes see kids quoting everything, because it's so much easier to do than paraphrasing or summarizing! But quotes should be used sparingly. You know those signs you can buy to hang around your house with quotes like "Whatever you are be a good one" by Abraham Lincoln or "Be who you are and say what you feel, because those who mind don't matter and those who matter don't mind" by Dr. Seuss? Those are wonderful quotes that make us stop and think about how seriously we do or don't take ourselves and life, right? So we hang them up in our living rooms or next to our beds as reminders to ourselves. The quotes you choose to put in your paper act in the same way. They are the ah-ha moments of academia. They are the words that make us stop and think about how to interpret our information. They're the insightful words that somebody deserves credit for. Sometimes we think if we can't paraphrase or summarize it's just easier to quote it, but that's not what quotes are for. Quotes are experts saying the truly important things that need to be painted onto the hypothetical sign you would hang in your essay.

But there's another kind of note I want you to think about—and that is reflective notes. While you are reading your materials, you will have thoughts

*pop into your head like—oh wow, this reminds me of . . . or questions like—
yeah, but if this happens, what about? . . . or statements like—I just don't
agree. Write these down! Your ideas and thoughts should be part of your notes,
because it is what will help you flesh out your paper and draw your
conclusions. If you are jotting down what is running through your mind while
you do this, you will have an easier time writing a final piece.*

*When you're taking notes, keep your mind tuned to the task at hand—how
do I support my message with facts? Do I retell information? Do I condense
it? Do I quote it? Or do I discuss connections or reactions to it?*

Are They Learning?

I was working with students who had had nearly two hours of independent
research time over two days when I sat down next to a boy. "Tell me everything you know," I said to him. After all, we had already gone over accessing
and assessing websites; I had created a LibGuide leading them to excellent
sources; we had reviewed note-taking. He should have, in two hours, had a
plethora of information on the colonization of his African country.

"I don't know anything," he stated.

"Well, let's start with the basics. Who colonized your country?" I asked.

He stared at me blankly. "I'm not sure. Britain or France, I think."

As I moved from student to student, similar, vague conversations
took place. They had EasyBibs started with their resources, they had lists
of bulleted notes, they had their assignments in front of them, they had
reliable resources open on their screens. When I scanned the room, it looked
like they were doing everything we had instructed them to do. Yet, each time
I sat down and asked, "Tell me what you know," they were caught off
guard.

One student grabbed his notes and started reading them to me. I interrupted. "Don't read me what your notes say, tell me what YOU know." He
asked me to give him ten minutes.

After they left class, I sat, reflecting, discouraged. I wanted to blame the
students, but I also know that if every single student in a class is not doing
what they need to do to be successful, I am responsible for some of that blame.
And so I sat and wondered, how can I get them back on track after this
railroaded research disaster? How do I help them actually learn while taking
notes?

The following day, when the students came in, they found large pieces
of bright paper with four index cards taped on them and my coveted collection

of Sharpies that they love to raid. Each index card had a question: *For what reason was your country colonized? What did life look like for the native inhabitants during colonization? How was the country liberated? What issues does your country struggle with today?* "Grab a color you like," I told them. "Grab some markers, and start writing what you know. If you don't know anything, write that. Be honest."

Students sprawled out on the tables and started jotting down what they could. They started digging out their notes and reading through them. As the other teacher and I circulated, we heard a lot of comments like, "I think I have more to look into" or "Wow, I didn't even pay attention to the part about that." When finished, they took out a piece of notebook paper and wrote down where they needed to focus during the class period that stretched ahead of them.

During research time, there was a different tone—a sense of purpose. They started asking us questions about what they were reading. They started being able to answer our questions. When there were five minutes left in class, they returned to their poster-sized notes and scribbled more information down. And then, again, they wrote on notebook paper what they needed to focus on over the weekend.

It was simple really, and I was disappointed in myself for not doing this kind of check in on day one. But it reminded me, once again, that we so often forget to teach explicitly about thinking and reflection. When we tell kids to go research their topic, they comply and walk through the paces that we have "trained" them to do. But how do we show them how to reflect on what they are finding? On reading for understanding? On finding purpose in their searches? These habits of mind must be taught daily in order for them to independently make meaning of their learning when they leave for college.

So what can we do to bring explicitness into the learning that needs to take place when taking notes?

- **Confer with students constantly.** Go to them—don't wait for them to come to you. Sometimes when students are working quietly, it is very easy for me to sit down and catch up on email, talk to a para about plans, or read papers. But only the most conscientious students who recognize they need help will approach me at that point. Instead, when we make daily conversations about the task at hand part of the normal routine, we get a better pulse on what they are learning. "Do you need any help?" rarely gets an affirmative answer. Instead, ask specific questions like: Why did you choose this topic? What is the most important thing you have read? What do you remember most? What does this mean today? Who are the important figures? What has been the most confusing part of your reading today?

- **Ask students to be active in their daily learning process.** Have them write entrance and exit slips—What do you plan to accomplish today and how are you going to do that? What did you accomplish today? What do you have left to do? Transition the ownership of their learning to them. Ask them to reflect on their habits—are they proud of their work today? Did they struggle with something? Did they use their time well? What would they do differently?

- **Ask students to stop what they are doing and write from time to time**. My students and I call these "brain dumps." Have them dump all of their knowledge out on paper. Sometimes, like we did with the colonization project, you can provide questions for them to answer. Other times, they can clump their own knowledge. Writing is thinking, and giving them the time to sit and think about what they know for a moment will help them be more efficient in moving forward in the process. After they have written and dumped out all of the information, ask them to find the holes—where do they need to focus next?

Explicit note instruction takes time. But in a world where people get their news from memes I, for one, will leave reminders for myself, in my next unit. Because the next time I sit next to a student and ask, "Tell me what you know," I want her to confidently look me in the eye and open the world.

 **TAKING A CLOSER LOOK**

Wendi Pillars

ESOL Brainchanger

Wendi Pillars is a National Board Certified teacher who has been teaching students with English as a second/foreign language needs in grades K-12, both stateside and overseas, for 21 years. She has also taught Algebra, History, Science, vocational classes, and Health and PE. In her book, *Visual Notetaking for Educators: A Teacher's Guide to Student Creativity*, she takes an honest look at note-taking strategies for students who wrestle with language and comprehension (all students at some point!), recognizing that many traditional methods aren't effective ways for some of our students to retain information. Using neuroscience to drive her practice, she gives her students techniques to access concepts in their research.

Here's what she says to those of us who are hesitant or nervous about incorporating visual note-taking in our practice:

> *One of the biggest concerns teachers have is simply how to get started with using visual notes in the classroom, especially if they're not comfortable with their own "drawing" skills.*
>
> *Sometimes a little convincing goes a long way. What better way to convince someone than to have them try it themselves? Here are seven ways you and your students can "see" the benefits of using visual note-taking within just a few minutes:*
>
> 1. ***Optimize your text for double duty.*** *Choose a short content-based text, not necessarily complex, but with detail. Ask students to scan or read the text then chunk it into sections. For each section, have them seek out key words or phrases, then represent what they read with quick sketches on sticky notes or a paper pre-folded into sections. Sometimes a blank piece of paper can be intimidating, so simple constraints can work wonders. This applies to the physical paper as well as time; providing 2–3 minutes per sketch at most ensures that the focus is on the thinking rather than the "art." Always emphasize "Process Over Pretty."*
>
> 2. ***Toss artistic fears out the window.*** *Ask students* **"How can we represent this with a sketch?"** *at pre-determined points in the learning. Have an idea yourself of both questions to ask and how you might sketch a given concept, but when a student suggests their idea(s), hand them the marker right away and support their efforts! Ironically, the worse YOU draw, the more inviting it is for students to try, the lower their affective filters drop, the more fun there is, and consequently, the better the learning sticks. (And a cool fact? Your brain only needs about 30% of a drawing to start making connections! It's very suggestible, so if you indicate whether your squiggly line is a road, a rope, or a wave, your brain will connect immediately!)*
>
> 3. ***Try a different media for listening practice.*** *For example, when introducing students to the idea of "fake news," first we* **listened** *to a TED Ed video. I stopped the video every 20 seconds or so (based on ideas, and keywords presented), for students to sketch. This helped them "hold" that information long enough to draw a representation, and anticipate the next idea. They shared main ideas of the video with a shoulder partner, using their sketches as an anchor for speaking. After sharing, we then* **watched** *the video, which is very visual and uses many sketches,*

so that students could confirm or revise their understanding. Keep it low-stakes, and for those who struggle, challenge them to write down or sketch at least one word from each video segment.

4. ***Share sketches*** *in small groups or whole class. Have volunteers share with a partner, or grouping to support the learning goals, to explain their thinking and add verbal detail to their sketches. Students will see immediately that even though they read, viewed or listened to the exact same text or media, their* **visual minds can think in very different pictures**. *They will also see how different details resonate with each other, driving home how readily we understand the same words through different lenses. This is also a great time to explain how the brain loves this type of challenge!*

5. ***Represent a single key term or phrase*** *before starting a unit, book, theme, or activity. Ask students to represent the word "research" with a quick sketch, and I promise you will gain invaluable insights into the level of their angst. Do they sketch themselves hiding in a corner, full of confidence, or full of confusion? How can you use those insights to proceed more effectively?*

6. ***Circulate through the room as they sketch***. *Even though it's 2–3 minutes at most, you will grasp an expedient realization of students' prior knowledge, questions they may have, levels of detail and their listening abilities. It's also the perfect time for organic conversations with your students about what they are drawing: "Can you tell me more about why you chose that image to represent _____?" *Note: Never judge a student's art. If something is questionable, simply ask the student to tell you more about it. Continually emphasize the thinking process.*

7. ***Extend its uses metacognitively.*** *How is this type of note-taking useful in other classes? Situations? Relate it to visualizing for success like athletes do. Rather than merely holding the visual in their mind, they take it a step further, and transfer the imagery to paper. Successful people visualize and write down their goals. In my class we sketch the best versions of ourselves, what we look like when we're successful. It's a powerful activity, and for many, it was the first time imagining their success with such detail, even when we used stick figures.*

Quotes my students have recently said about using visual notes:

"Drawing helps slow down and give us an idea of what will happen when we don't understand all the language."

"Sketching helps me learn what I don't know. You see what I don't understand then you tell me information in a different way."

#tldnr?

"Teaching note-taking is difficult, and requiring it is time-consuming."

"Good note-taking strategies are the key to avoiding unintentional plagiarism."

"When explicitly teaching note-taking, I have four non-negotiables: 1. Notes must be handwritten. 2. Notes must be in your own words. 3. Notes must be written in phrases, not complete sentences. 4. Notes need to be tracked back to each source."

"It is important to show students a variety of different methods of note-taking strategies and let them determine which techniques will best help them access and remember the information."

"When we tell kids to go research their topic, they comply and walk through the paces that we have 'trained' them to do. But how do we show them how to reflect on what they are finding? On reading for understanding? On finding purpose in their searches? These habits of mind must be taught daily in order for them to independently make meaning of their learning when they leave for college."

#tryonething

Model note-taking strategies with your students.

When it's time to have students take notes, pull out the old overhead projector or the new document camera, and unpack the process in front of their very eyes. Open a book or a website and make your thinking about how to put the right words down transparent for them. When they see you work through the process, they will have a better understanding of how to take notes themselves.

6

Putting It All Together

Organizing the Parts of Your Research Paper

Every winter I escape New England winters and go out to Death Valley to hike, camp, and breathe in solitude. Way out, at the end of a 26-mile washboard road that takes about three hours to drive, sits Ubehebe Peak. Nearly 3,000 feet from the desert floor, the peak is a pointed pinnacle that allows summiters to peer over to the Saline Valley on the other side. I had read about the 6-mile roundtrip hike, and decided it was a good way to spend a February afternoon. But when I parked at its base, fear weaseled its way into my heart. How on earth was I going to climb that? I am terrified of edges and falling, and this looked like a straight scramble to the top. I began to doubt myself.

But when I threw my pack over my shoulders and grabbed some water, I discovered that the route to the top was an old miner's trail that wound itself in hairpin turns up the side of the mountain. Each stretch of trail took on a small incline before winding itself around in the opposite direction. The hike, broken up into these small sections, wasn't nearly as scary as I'd thought. In fact, it was perfectly manageable.

So many times I watch students open up a blank document and start typing while they are doing their research. "What are you writing?" I'll ask them. "My research paper," they respond incredulously, as though I have not even been in the same room this whole time. "But how do you know what to write if you aren't done researching?" I'll ask. I still haven't gotten an answer that satisfies me. When students do that, they are me, standing at the bottom of Ubehebe, thinking I have to scramble on hands and knees to get to the top—they are just tackling it the only way they know how—straight

Source: Discovery Channel

Klondike Region
-mountainous
-no roads/paths
-rivers high/dangerous
-very hot summers—short!
-very long, cold winters—60!

Different ways to get there
1. Yukon River   -2K miles
                        -dangerous rapids (White Horse)
                        -swampy areas with mosquitoes
2. Dead Horse Gulch
                        -3K horses and mules died
                        -Bodies left -blocked path
3. Chilkoot Pass
                        -fastest
                        -inexpensive
                        -avalanche risk
                        -no animals, too steep
                        -carried gear
                        -snow, sleet, blinding sun
                        -in winter: stairs carved
                        -Golden Stairs
                        -heavy packs, hunched over
                        -lines of thousands of miners

Figure 6.1 An example of my notes that I use with students

up. They haven't seen that there's a mule trail yet. They don't see that there's an easier, windier way.

Telling students they need to write a research paper often feels like telling them to summit a tall, pointy, impossibly difficult peak in the middle of the desert. I've seen the fear of writing research lay itself out in students' eyes, clear as day. What we have to show them is that when it's broken up into tiny stretches that gently push at each stage, it's not as hard as they think. A big hike is the accumulation of a bunch of small steps. A research paper is the same thing.

Organizing Information

When students have taken all of their notes, it's difficult for them to understand how to turn those notes into an essay. There's a leap there from unpolished work to polished work. The first thing we have to show them is that organizing that information is the most important groundwork they can lay for their writing.

Here's what I tell students:

I know writing the essay seems like the hardest part to you, but really you have done all of the difficult legwork. It is just going to get easier from here on in—IF you take this next small step: organizing your notes. Look at all of the information you have in front of you. There's a lot, right? But it's not going to all go in one part of the essay. It's not going to all go into the essay in the order you wrote it down.

So look through your information. First, I want you to categorize it. What are the different topics you have? How do these notes clump together to work together? You can do this a couple of different ways. If you used index cards, you can find a big space and move them into separate piles. If you used Cornell notes, you can cut them up into pieces and do the same thing as the notecards. Or, you can highlight each topic a certain color. That goes for any kind of note-taking. Either physically move them or color code them. But look for patterns and subtopics.

When that is done, you then have to think about the order the information needs to be introduced to your reader in order to make sense. You wouldn't talk about the effects of a flood before you talked about the storm itself, right? So sort through that information—which pieces do you need first? How do you want to introduce new material? From there, tape your cards together, type your notes, or handwrite everything out again. I'll be completely honest: when I do this step, I rewrite everything while I organize it. It helps me remember my information and it makes everything clean and orderly.

If you take the time and organize your information here, I promise, the writing will be easy.

I do not require formal, typed outlines that are perfect to the very piece of punctuation. I tell students they certainly can make outlines, but lists, bullets, or checkboxes all work as well. It's not so much about the Roman numerals as it is about the ideas being laid out in a way that will make sense when writing.

Thesis Statements

My daughter was applying for a post-graduate research scholarship when she let out a big, defeated sigh, and asked, "How do I write what a thesis is if I haven't done my research yet?"

This is a question I ask teachers all the time when they insist on having a thesis statement written ahead of the reading and note-taking. Sure, in situations of post-grad research like what my daughter is undertaking or doctoral proposals, the thesis acts as a kind of hypothesis—it's a theory or a premise and it's based on preliminary research they've done in writing a proposal. But in middle and high school, the process is different. Students don't have the background knowledge necessary to write a thesis, which acts as the main idea of the research—the thrust of what the rest of the paper will support. How can that be done on limited knowledge? I stand behind the belief that the thesis is written *after* students have read through, taken notes on, and organized all of their information. (There is of course, the exception of the forthright argument paper. If a student is writing a pro-death penalty essay, she will easily be able to state that the death penalty is necessary. Argumentative assertions are much simpler to write than theses that synthesize multiple ideas to conclude a larger idea.)

The thesis statement should also be a well-crafted sentence; not a list of topics. For example, "Despite initial failures, Steve Jobs' experiences propelled him to change not only the music industry, but how ordinary people live their lives" is a better sentence than "Steve Jobs changed the music industry and how people live." I provide students with a list of "sentence starter words" like despite, because, while, during, although, as, etc. I show them the power of the appositive phrase (a noun phrase that adds information to another noun. Example: Steve Jobs, an unprecedented innovator . . .). I show them how writing with a subordinating conjunction (like because, although, while, etc.) at the beginning of the sentence automatically helps build a sentence rich with information. Think of what makes a good sentence, figure out the grammar behind it, and then explicitly show them what good writing looks like.

Here's what I tell students:

> *A thesis is a fancy word that tries to intimidate us. New vocabulary works best when we can file it away in a folder in our mental filing cabinet that is already filled with words we are comfortable with. But thesis? There's nothing to connect that word to—and so it is intimidating and foreign to us. So let's just unpack it.*

> *A thesis statement is a fancy way of saying Main Idea of your Research. So let's go back to your original essential question. Now that you've done all of your research, you should be able to answer that. It's what you can conclude after synthesizing all of the information from your reading. It's what you want to prove. What you want to back up. It's a taste of what you're about to unfold in your essay. The easiest way to start is to answer your question. If you had to boil your entire research down and answer that question in one sentence, what would it be? How would it represent your work?*

> *Writing this thesis statement can be hard—you don't want to give all of your information in it, but you do want to introduce your main points. You want it to sound sophisticated and fluid, but simple and clear—it should be beautiful writing, not a list of ideas. It might take a couple of tries. As you write it, I'll give you feedback.*

> *You want your thesis statement to be a tall, proud, beautiful sentence that sets the tone for your entire project. Try starting with one of the sentence starters or by using an appositive phrase. Try a few different ways of saying what you want to say. When you are assessing and critiquing that sentence, ask yourself—does this stand on its own? Is this worthy of representing all of my work? Does it lay the groundwork for my audience? Scribble different ideas down—don't worry about getting it right that first time. It will come. For now, they are just words on paper for you to play with. If it's not perfect, it's okay.*

I always model the thesis writing process for students. Just as I modeled coming up with an essential question, I model how to come up with that answer. I don't pre-write it before the students are in front of me, because I want them to see me struggle. I scratch drafts out, I comment on words that I don't think are strong enough, I work through the process and let them chime in with suggestions. When they give me feedback and help me improve, they are more accepting of being on the other end.

During class, I try to give students time to write their thesis statements and I circulate the room and meet with each one to provide them with guidance. The reality is, however, that there is not enough time to meet with every student or even to give them the opportunity to work on it. When this is the case, I create a document and share it with each class member. They write their theses in their designated space and I make comments on each one. The beauty of this is that they can see what others are doing for inspiration of how to write.

Writing the Paper—Structure

Once the organization has been built and the thesis has been fully developed, it is time to write. This is that pointy-peaked mountain that scares all writers of all ages, but if we've walked them through the previous pieces, we've laid the trail for them—now we just have to show them how to get to it. There are three parts of the essay I want students to think about as they begin writing: the introduction, the body paragraphs, and the conclusion.

Here's what I tell students:

Introduction

Think of how you are as a reader before you start writing. If the piece doesn't grab your attention, you don't give it too much of a commitment, right? Especially if it's nonfiction. There is nothing more boring than boring nonfiction! But there's nothing cooler than nonfiction that engages its readers. You want your audience to read your first few lines and be hooked. You want them to be interested in what lies ahead. You want them to want to hear your work. So don't start with something that sounds like a line from an encyclopedia. Start with a story. Or a really startling statistic. Begin with a fact that entices me to know more. Build a scene—bring me on location. Create a hypothetical situation that takes me outside of my own perspective. But whatever you do, grab me by the shirt collars and make me want to read your paper!

Attention getting is the beginning of your introductory paragraph and your thesis statement is the end of that introductory paragraph. Which means between those two things you will have to transition. You'll have to move fluidly from the hook to the main thrust of the paper. When all of those components are in place: an attention getter, transition pieces, and a thesis statement, you've done two things: 1. You've gotten me excited about your topic and 2. You've let me know what the purpose of this research is.

Body Paragraphs

You've already sorted through your notes and organized them into topics. Now those notes are going to become your paragraphs. You will need a topic sentence like, "The multiple avenues of reaching the Klondike region to search for gold offered up life-threatening dangers." This tells me that in this paragraph there will be information about the dangers of getting to the Klondike. From there, I will incorporate my notes, composing sentences from them. Sometimes I will combine facts in one sentence; sometimes I will add my own voice and reflection.

Here is where I use my notes to model writing from them. Again, I do not pre-write my paragraph; I compose in front of them so they can see that it doesn't always come easy. As I write in front of the students, I talk aloud. I tell them when I'm unhappy with a word I've used. I contemplate about the order of my facts and rearrange them. I show them my thinking process. Laying out writing as an explicit act—making it transparent—demystifies it for our students.

When I am done writing the paragraph, I ask students what they noticed about my writing process. They recognize that it is a recursive process; that

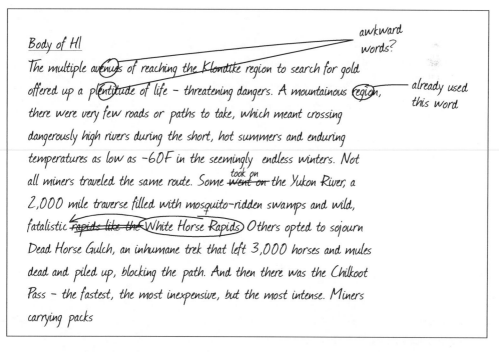

Figure 6.2 Writing from notes in front of my students

it isn't perfect; that I bring more than just a list of facts to the paper. But what I see in them is more confidence in their ability to get their writing done—they just watched me write a paragraph in ten minutes, and now know that they can do that too. That they have the same mule path laid out in front of them.

So heavy, they ~~were~~ climbed the nearly vertical trail, hunched over, traversed the
long
pass in/lines. Exposed to avalanches, they climbed through snow and sleet. In the
they carved
winter/stairs into the pass, naming them the Golden Stairs. In the summer,
(Discovery)
the sun's reflection off the snow was so bright it literally left some men blind. No matter
which route the men, ~~hungry for~~ lured by the call of gold, decided to take, they had to
ask themselves the question, "Is the prospect of wealth worth not only discomfort or
injury, but the possibility of death?" For many, the answer was simple: yes.

Figure 6.3 Writing from notes in front of my students

What did you notice watching me write?

- Kept going even when not satisfied
- Added adjectives and better words
- Not just what notes said
- Different kinds of sentences
- Rearranged facts—didn't necessarily stick with original order
- Had some sentences w/no facts—talking about them instead
- Felt like you were talking to us
- Topic sentence and concluding sentence

Figure 6.4 What my students notice about my research writing process

The Conclusion

Writing the conclusion is often the hardest part of the essay—I mean, you've already said everything you want to say, right? But this is the important part. It's the drink of milk after a big plate of spaghetti and meatballs. It's the feeling you get after you jump into the shower after a game. It's brushing your teeth before bed. It wraps it all up and makes the reader feel satisfied. There are a couple of things you should include in your conclusion:

1. *If this is an argument paper, what are the solutions you are proposing? What is the course of action you want your reader to take?*

2. *If you are proving another point, what conclusions are you drawing? Think of a science experiment—You've watched a flame turn blue. You've described what happened and now you can draw conclusions— there are gas molecules that have changed color because the flame is very hot. You aren't repeating information; you're drawing your conclusions based on the information you've given. You're reiterating your thesis and using all of your body paragraphs to support your final conclusions.*

3. *When you are done writing, read your entire paper aloud. How does that ending sound? Does it feel like it wraps it up? Finalizes? Does it end with your voice and your final thoughts? Or does it feel choppy? Abrupt? Often, hearing it helps us as writers discover what is missing.*

 **TAKING A CLOSER LOOK**

Kathleen Murdough

Social Studies

Kathleen Murdough is a ninth grade Social Studies teacher for a rural regional high school. Her students, coming in from five different middle schools, often show up to her heterogenous classes with varying skills in the classroom. When writing essays in history class, students often turned in either big blocks of text with no paragraph breaks or random paragraph blocks that adhered to a five-sentence-paragraph formula. She had students across the spectrum. Some simply did not know how to properly paragraph an essay while others took part in "academic vomiting"—taking all of the information and being unable to narrow it down to answer the question being asked. She discovered that many students were not practiced at identifying relevant information and inserted all of their notes, despite pertinence. Her higher-achieving students had fallen into the dangerous trap of longer always being better. No matter the ability of the student, she realized that her students had some difficult habits to overcome.

Here's what Kathleen told me:

> To combat these problems, I started to teach them how to outline on index cards. Each index card represents a part of the essay. So they will have an index card for their introduction; index cards for their body paragraphs; and one for the conclusion. This helps students organize what goes where so they can clearly visualize it when they start to write the essay. I explain to students, "This is where you stop because you've included everything that's on the index card. If you're ready to move onto the next index card, you're starting a new paragraph. Because index cards have a space limitation, this also helps with avoiding overwriting.
>
> We have students try many different methods of note-taking, so they come to the writing process with a bunch of research in some form. And then I start with the thesis. I tell them, "Yes, this is part of the introduction, but it's not the introduction." Writing a full introduction is hard for them—they just want to start with their thesis. I have them write the thesis at the bottom or on the back of their first index card. This reminds them that other information needs to be included here. I ask them to think about the claim they are making and to imagine that if the audience is entirely new to their topic, what do they need to include? How do you introduce and explain your topic? What things does your audience have to know before you can make this claim?
>
> Teaching students to organize the body paragraphs is also tricky, because they are often used to formulaic writing and they believe that there should only be three or five body paragraphs. To combat this, I have them to go back to their thesis—reexamine that claim they made, and then look through their details in their research. I ask them to clump all the details that are on one related topic together and rewrite them on the card. If they find that they are starting to talk about another topic, then they need another card. It's an interesting process to watch them sort out their information, and takes more guidance than you would think. I move throughout the classroom and check in on them, but I also have them check each others' details.
>
> Questions I ask them while I work alongside them include:
>
> • Does the information on your index card have a common thread?
>
> • Are all of your facts on one card related to the same idea?
>
> • Do these facts match up with and prove your thesis?
>
> Before I have them do this on their own, I do one on the board and talk myself through it. Then we have a student do one on the board as well. Learning this process is more about explicit demonstration than light bulb language.

Part of sorting through the facts for the body paragraphs also includes eliminating some information. Sometimes they have cool facts, but it's not the point they are trying to make. Getting kids to depart from "cool facts" can be difficult—and sometimes they end up actually changing their thesis because their facts have moved them in another direction. This can be a frustrating process, but shows them that real research is about saying something valuable.

In text citations must be happening at this point, as well. If it's going to be cited in the essay, it must be cited on the card. It makes everything so much easier. If they don't believe me, they do after they have to go back and find the source again.

When we get to the conclusion, that's the hardest part. That's the part they say they've never really understood. Often, they repeat word for word what they've already said. I'll tell them, "Sure, you're not going to add new information in the conclusion, but the way you say it has to be new. Go back to your thesis and ask yourself how you can phrase it another way." While it seems very formulaic, I tell writers who are really wrestling with their conclusion to count up how many body paragraphs they have. They need at least this many sentences in their conclusion as they summarize their main points. It's a starting point, not a requirement. Most writers are able to move away from this as the year progresses.

The idea of "essay" is so overwhelming. Getting anything on a page can be paralyzing. This practice has helped me ease those fears while also guiding students to write concisely and focused. It lays the basics for the rest of high school that they will need.

#tldnr?

"Telling students they need to write a research paper often feels like telling them to summit a tall, pointy, impossibly difficult peak in the middle of the desert."

"Organizing [their] information is the most important groundwork they can lay for their writing."

"The thesis is written after students have read through, taken notes on, and organized all of their information . . . and should be a well-crafted sentence, not a list of topics."

"There are three parts of the essay I want students to think about as they begin writing: the introduction, the body paragraphs, and the conclusion."

"Laying out writing as an explicit act—making it transparent—demystifies it for our students."

#tryonething

Give students a list of starter words to start theses with.

Show students that when they start sentences with words like while, as, after, although, despite, if, before, because, etc. it automatically helps them build a richer sentence they can fit more information into.

7

The Part That's Never ExCITEing
Making Works Cited
an Easier Accomplishment

Teaching students how to cite properly might be the most-skipped part of research instruction in the everyday classroom (I guiltily confess it is the step I have found myself most tempted to skip in any research project). A combination of new technology that makes the cumbersome process more manageable and the time it takes to work through all of the necessary components adds up to teachers skimming or skipping the process, hoping that their students will remember what was taught the last time.

Works Cited

I am as guilty of this as anyone. Creating a Works Cited is not fun. It's my least favorite part of research. Yet, it is also critical that students understand the work they have pulled from must be accounted for. Respecting intellectual property is often a difficult concept for students who have grown up with information, music, artwork, and writing readily available. The lines feel blurry to them.

In fact, I am always surprised that students often don't understand the meaning behind the title: Works Cited. I tell middle school students, in particular, that "works" is a piece of work: writing, video, interview . . . it's crafted material. "Cited" means you used it in your writing. (Personally, I prefer Works Consulted because sometimes we read information that helps build our knowledge, but we don't actually end up outright using it, but I know that's not mainstream.) Then we move into the logistics of building one. Which isn't as easy as one would think.

A seventh grade history teacher and I had earmarked a day for all students to create their Works Cited. They had used a mixture of media in their recent country project: pictures, books, databases, websites, and video. We had had them keep track of everything along the way and anticipated that one 45-minute class period would be ample time.

We were wrong.

As we went through the steps, me modeling with my own research project on Iceland, we found students falling behind and not knowing where to go. They didn't understand what the term MLA meant. They didn't know what a URL was. They couldn't tell the difference between a website title and a website page title. They didn't know where to look to see if a photographer was credited. Some of them assuredly jumped on easybib.com, telling us they had done all this before, and started creating their own Works Citeds, citing everything as a website and not recognizing the nuances of databases or online photographs, and then getting frustrated that they had to delete those citations.

Once we got everything into a document, they didn't know the rules of Works Cited: everything has to be the same font and size, and entries have to be alphabetized. So when they pulled a generated citation from a database and tried to integrate it with their EasyBib material, they didn't recognize that they had to move things around, and then they weren't sure how to cut the citation out and paste it in another place. Some students tried to un-indent the second line of each citation because it looked "weird."

We knew they had been taught how to create Works Citeds in elementary school, but everything we had assumed about their prior knowledge to citing was wrong.

By the end of the first period, we felt like we had already put in a full, exhaustive day of terrible teaching. Their Works Citeds were not finished, and we were pretty sure that tomorrow they wouldn't be able to find them because in the state of being overwhelmed, we forgot to remind them to title their Google Doc as a Works Cited.

We all have bad days in the classroom. And while I hate to fail on precious student time, I am reminded that failure has its purpose in life: to teach us what sucked so we don't do it again. A quick, post-class, reflective conference, before second period, helped us identify what went wrong and adjust the lesson. By the final periods of the day, our students were leaving with a completed, titled, fully formatted Works Cited saved on their computers. We triumphed. So what did we learn today about teaching bibliography skills?

We need to teach kids how to read their resources for citation information.

Remember when we (and by "we" I mean anybody over the age of 30) used to have to type our Works Cited by hand? We not only had to know where commas and periods and italics went, but we had to know book titles, publishers, dates, cities, etc. While sites like EasyBib make remembering the formatting component obsolete, they still require the writer to look for publication information. Students still need to know how to look for titles, publishers, dates, and cities. In fact, I would even argue that they have to know more information than we did "back in the day" because they now have access to YouTube videos, online databases and encyclopedias, oodles of online artwork, let alone websites. They need to understand where to look for authors, publishers, titles, etc. because sometimes EasyBib doesn't pick them up. Explicit instruction on how to do this is key. Subscriptions like Noodle Tools don't automatically generate the citation; instead they require students to manually import the information.

Regardless of which tool students use, ask them to double check all of the information and punctuation. Show them how to go back to different kinds of resources to find the information they need. Double checking their information and tracking it back to the source will ensure they have accurate records.

We need to teach students that there are different rules for different kinds of sources.

Our students often think that if it is on their computer screen, it is a website. They don't see the difference between an eBook or a database. They don't realize that an online video is cited differently than an online photograph. They don't realize that an online photograph is different than an online painting. They often think they can cite Google Images rather than the site that carries a picture itself or that a URL link to that picture is the correct way to cite it. Show students the "59 Other Options" on EasyBib. Give them class time to work on these so you can help them with questions.

Teachers need to know the rules, too.

If we don't know the rules, then we aren't catching students' errors in their citations. We need to be able to look at a Works Cited and say, "Hmmm. I think there's something wrong here. Let's go back in and edit that together." I have seen many wrongly formatted Works Citeds be handed in and get "okay-ed" by the teacher. If you are unsure of what all of the components that go into a Works Cited are, enlist your librarian for help!

Students need time to cite correctly.

When we don't, we implicitly let students know that it is not important. When we accept any version they have created (I've seen them handed in numbered, bulleted, as a list of URLs, etc.), we also send that message. When we give students the time to work on this with us, it also allows them to start asking really important questions. I worked with one student who had used a bunch of YouTube videos. He had cited them all by just typing in the general YouTube home site address and not differentiating between each video, so every citation had the same exact information. What this told me was he went to YouTube and nothing else. This opened up a great conversation between us about where to look for that information.

Kids need practice.

Teaching Works Cited cannot be a one-time practice. Explicit citation lessons must be part of each project, allowing for student questions and struggles. "Back in the day" I always had to pull out my Diana Hacker to figure out how to cite a book with two editors. I simply could not remember what information was needed. Our kids need similar guides and frequent practice at accessing guides. There are lots of great online guides right now, but the OWL at Purdue is a solid favorite.

Technology does not neatly solve all problems. While putting together a Works Cited feels easier to us, because we don't have to remember the formatting intricacies, we are often failing to teach students the content of what goes into a Works Cited. We need to know the rules, give ample time to practice, and show students how to read resources for publication information. EasyBib and other citing machines are miraculous tools, yes. But they do not replace our students' thinking. In fact, our students have much more to think about when addressing issues of citation than we ever did.

Annotated Bibliographies

"Tell me about this source," I asked Katherine as she showed me her information for her Psychology project. "Why did you pick it?" Katherine was researching whether people who are considered to be more beautiful are more successful in their careers. The source she had started taking notes on was a study on the connection between physical attractiveness and eating disorders. "Because it is about being beautiful," she responded. "Yes, but does the information in the study intersect with your essential question at all? Tell me what this article is about." She sat in silence for a few minutes. "I'm not entirely sure," she responded.

It was at this moment that I realized I had failed to ask Katherine and the other kids to be metacognitive with her resources. I never asked them to think about what kind of information exactly in this and how could it be used? Yes, we had done the CRAAP test, but this was a red flag that we needed to look a little closer at the R—relevancy. We needed to be writing annotated bibliographies.

An annotated bibliography has two components to it:

1. The citation itself.

2. A short paragraph (usually 150 words or less) that:

   - Gives a description of what the resource is. Is it a primary source? A current event?
   - Gives a brief summary of the source. What is it about? What information is valuable?
   - Discusses the author and source. Who is it written by? What authority do they have?
   - Assesses the source. How does it help you? Why is it worth using?

Slowing down to do this certainly adds time, but the benefits are monumental. While the purpose of an annotated bibliography is in the interest of the reader, I believe the metacognitive process of closely examining and reflecting upon resources behooves our students' learning even more. It encourages students to slow down and really understand what kind of material they are looking at. Instead of just saying—hey, this is great information! They have to first say—Hey, wait. This is some guy's blog who has no credentials on his page. Let me see if I can find this information somewhere else. It also encourages students to determine which sources are useful for them and which ones are not. It's another metacognitive step in the research process that helps our students think like researchers in extended situations.

Examples of annotated bibliographies are readily available online, with clear examples on sites like Cornell University Library Website and the OWL at Purdue. Most citation generators have a spot on their site where researchers can easily add their annotations.

Here's how I introduce annotated bibliographies to students:

Annotated bibliographies are often expected in college and university classes. But I'm going to ask you to start working on them now, because they help you in thinking about your collected resources. They make you a more reflective, deliberate researcher. As you start collecting material, I want you to ask yourself some simple questions:

- *What is this source about?*
- *Is it any good?*
- *Is it helpful?*
- *Why or why not?*
- *What information is included?*

A lot of these questions are questions you use when choosing your information, right? They're part of the CRAAP test. So the annotated bibliography is just taking your resource assessment to the next level—writing it down and reflecting on it. At the end of your citation, you should have at least a paragraph reflecting on the content, credibility, and relevancy of the source. Think of it as a conversation with your reader, one where you're saying— this is what it's about, this is why it's reliable, and this is why it's relevant and important to my research. This frames your moving forward with your work and really helps you decide which resources you need to include. It might seem like extra work in the beginning, but it helps focus your reading, ultimately making you a more efficient researcher.

Parenthetical Citations . . . (When?)

"You only have to cite information that is not common knowledge," I told a group of junior history students. Samantha raised her hand. "What would you consider common knowledge?" she asked. "Well, I have always been told that if it appears in three sources, it's common knowledge. So something like the inaugural date of George Washington . . . that's in almost everything you read on his presidency."

She looked at me curiously. "But with the Internet, things are used and written about and reprinted all the time . . . so isn't everything common knowledge now?"

She has a point. Students have great difficulty in determining what common knowledge is—because all of it is new to them. None of it is common. So how do we help them figure it out?

The MIT Academic Integrity Handbook reminds us that these things are NOT common knowledge ever:

- Datasets generated by you or others.
- Statistics obtained from sources such as the US Census Bureau and the Bureau of Labor Statistics.

- References to studies done by others.
- Reference to specific dates, numbers, or facts the reader would not know unless s/he had done the research.

(MIT)

Since that conversation with Samantha, I've changed my response. Here's what I tell students now:

> *We all know that when we quote a writer or a speaker, we have to credit them in our writing. But when we use somebody else's ideas in a summary or a paraphrase to build on our own ideas, we have to give credit to them then, too. But, here's the tricky part—you don't have to cite everything. If it's common knowledge, it's something that most people know. But what does that mean—most people? Who are most people? I mean, if you are writing about fishing lures for a fishing magazine, what those people generally know might be very different than if you were writing about a new medical discovery for a pharmaceutical company. "Most people" has a fluid definition—it can change by culture, geography, hobby, field of study or practice . . . so common knowledge is partially determined by what you know, but also what your audience knows. It's a tricky balance. If I'm writing about the Emancipation Proclamation, I don't have to cite that Abraham Lincoln wrote it—that's common knowledge for United States' citizens. But what if I didn't know that? What if my audience didn't know that? That's where the tricky part comes into play. And that's where if you do see it in every source you're reading about—if it seems like nonchalant, conversational kind of information, then it's common knowledge. If you're not sure, ask a teacher while you're writing. We'll help you talk through it. And, at any point, when you're doubting, the rule of thumb is: over-citing is far better than plagiarizing.*

Not Just MLA!

MLA is, by far, the most used style guide in middle and high school research. But often, students do not know why they are using it or what it means. When they enter college and are asked to use APA in some of their classes, they are overwhelmed. Starting everyone using MLA is a systematic, routine way to expose students to citation guides. But as they get older and break off into specialized classes like Religion, Business, Sociology, Nursing, Criminology and Forensic Sciences, or Psychology, they are ready to be shown how different style guides are used for different fields of study. We need to introduce students to the different methods of citation guides before they are asked to master them in college.

Teaching citations is certainly not the fun part of teaching students how to research. It lacks the wonder and excitement that is infused with curiosity. It's about protocol and order. It's akin to having to organize your spices while doing a kitchen renovation. But it's important work that teaches our students how to responsibly document their academic practices.

TAKING A CLOSER LOOK

Jessica Ferren

Psychology

Jess Ferren, a certified school librarian and Social Studies teacher, has been showing her high school students how to create annotated bibliographies for 20 years. We sat down to talk about her practice and I was able to ask her some questions about why she immerses students in this practice.

When and why did you start asking students to annotate their bibliographies?

As an undergrad I had a professor who required his students to annotate their sources for a presentation and I realized that it really helped me be thoughtful about my research, so as long as I've been teaching I've required an annotated bibliography for my semester long research paper.

How do you frame that conversation with them?

It's always the first step in a research assignment. They determine their research question, but they don't know if they'll be able to answer it without finding out what's out there for research. I sell the annotated bibliography to them as an eventual time saver. Most of us can relate to finding something that looks promising but when digging in, it doesn't go where we expected. We discuss how doing that screening right at the beginning is a way to begin to weed out the irrelevant info and questionable sources so that when they sit down to begin the writing process, they're already in good shape. It also provides enough exposure to the topic and the relevant research to determine a possible direction as their thesis is taking shape. It also provides a first chance to be sure they've chosen a topic they genuinely want to pursue. For example, lots of times kids want to research dreams for their psychology thesis, but once they begin to dig in, they realize that the research doesn't go where they think it will.

What difficulties do they have in doing this?

The biggest difficulty kids have is generally determining credibility. This can be a challenge for all of us and the kids haven't always been asked to do this explicitly.

How do you see this practice benefiting your students' research habits?

It benefits students mainly because it requires them to think and engage with information. They are very used to restating information, but having to explicitly figure out what's useful from a source and why a source is or isn't trustworthy is a much more complex and intellectually challenging task. Obviously, most people aren't going to be writing research papers forever, but we all need to be critical consumers of information and that's perhaps one of the most important life skills I can help them learn! It seems with each passing day we see more and more just how essential, and often missing, skill this is.

Has research changed over the years for your students? Have you noticed if annotated bibliographies help them navigate the newer landscapes?

Well it's certainly changed since the days of the card catalog! Access has made the task both easier and more challenging. I have found that requiring an annotated bibliography has caused kids to be more willing to use online databases since the screening has been partially done. And once they've used them, they realize what a useful tool they are and begin to realize what a valuable resource they are and they begin to use them without prodding from me!

#tldnr?

"We need to teach kids how to read their resources for citation information . . . [and] that there are different rules for different kinds of sources."

"Students need time to cite correctly."

"While the purpose of an annotated bibliography is in the interest of the reader, I believe the metacognitive process of closely examining and reflecting upon resources behooves our students' learning even more."

"Over-citing is far better than plagiarizing."

"We need to introduce students to the different methods of citation guides before they are asked to master them in college."

#tryonething

Ask students to create an annotated bibliography.

As students collect their sources early in the process, have them write annotations assessing the credibility and usability of each one.

8

Beyond the Essay

How to Incorporate Podcasts, PSAs, and Other Valuable Projects Into the Classroom

Don't get bogged down by the research essay! While it's the most traditional student research product, there are other great ways for students to practice and incorporate their research skills. This chapter is meant to jumpstart new ideas and encourage you to think outside of the essay box!

Podcasts

Description
Students delve into a topic and write and record a script. It can be a formal, polished podcast fashioned after an NPR podcast or a conversational podcast like *Harry Potter as a Sacred Text*. Either way, students collect their research much as they would for an essay, but then incorporate it into a narrative. Students love making podcasts—they feel timely, ready for an audience, publishable, and engaging.

How-to
Students start podcast research much like they would traditional research—presearching, asking questions, taking notes. But when it comes to the organizing and writing portion, things are a little different, because podcasts incorporate more narrative components in them. Have them critically listen to other podcasts as examples.

As students listen to the podcasts, ask them to pay attention to music, narrative elements, interviews, and research components. How are they seamlessly melded into the craft of a podcast? As they listen as producers, they will begin to piece together their own ideas of how to bring their content alive. They will need to write out a script and practice before making a final recording. Products can be uploaded to iTunes or shared on the school website for a greater audience.

CREATING PODCASTS	
Great podcasts to use as exemplars:	Things to remember when recording:
<ul><li>Nate DiMeo's *The Memory Palace*</li><li>*Science Vs*</li><li>*60 Second Science*</li><li>*Civics 101*</li><li>*This American Life*</li><li>*Revisionist History*</li><li>*Invisibilia*</li></ul>	<ul><li>Record in a room that has good acoustics. This doesn't mean you need top notch equipment! Sitting in a closet or under a table with a big heavy quilt, talking into a smartphone often makes the best recording studio.</li><li>Practice!</li><li>Be sure to record separate pieces in the same location so as to have similar background ambiance.</li></ul>
Free software to use for editing:	Free music to use:
<ul><li>Audacity</li><li>Twisted Wave</li><li>Garageband</li><li>Soundation</li></ul>	<ul><li>Free Music Archive</li><li>Audionautics</li><li>Jamendo Music</li><li>CCTrax</li></ul>

PSAs

Description

A Public Service Announcement is a great way for students to do short research pieces on issues that concern them in almost any area of study. A PSA can be recorded the same as a podcast; it can be made into a short video clip; or it can be a visual graphic. Students would have to determine who their audience is and how they will best reach them.

How-to

Ask students to identify a societal problem in your field of study to research. The research for these is shorter and more condensed—they need to know what the problem is, why it's a problem, and determine why their audience should care and what could be done about it. They then need to look at samples of PSAs and break down the components—they should be aesthetically engaging, simple, clever, and appealing to our emotions. They are not pages of facts or a ten-minute video. Have students define their main message and what material they will include. The power of the PSA is that the creator has to be concise and focused to get as much convincing information across in a short amount of time or space.

Websites

Description

Websites are great places for students to publish their work for a greater audience. If it's a large writing project, they can include certain components like their essential question and their annotated bibliography on the website (Check out Newton High School's Capstone Project websites that their students build in Newton, MA). Another option is to have a class website that embraces a larger focus and each student publishes his or her research on its own page.

How-to

Decide the focus and scope of the research and either set up the website that students can add their pages to or have students set individual websites up. Wix, Google Sites, WordPress, Blogger, and Weebly all have easy themes for beginner website builders. Students then post their ongoing or final research on the website. They also need to pay attention to layout, design, aesthetics, while always keeping authentic audience in mind.

Community Awareness

Description

Having a real audience always makes research more relevant and accessible for students. Students can research a community issue, a charitable organization/event, or any topic and find a place for it to be on display for the community to access. One year my students researched the Holocaust and all of their research was put on display (longer pieces were made available through QR codes) at the town library alongside books that had to do with World War II and the Holocaust. Patrons came in and were immersed in a book display filled with student research to capture their attention. One teacher I worked with had her students research places around their town for their 250th birthday celebration. They made laminated signs with a quote from the research and a QR code that linked to the student work and placed them around the town.

How-to

Before embarking on the research, have students brainstorm ways they can get this information out to other members of their community. Maybe it is a dinner at the school; a large display before entering a school event; or space at a historical society, library, town hall, theatre, or bookstore. Reach out and ask if this is something the organization may be willing to house. A community is generally excited to showcase and celebrate what their schools are studying. Be sure that students understand their audience and that their displays are not heavy with solid text (this is why we always linked the papers with QR codes) and are visually engaging. Once the research is done, deliver (or request the help of parent volunteers) and set up for a designated amount of time.

Debate

Description

Students *love* to debate. Open up Facebook—*everybody* loves to debate! Because of this, it is critical for our kids to understand that their opinions are not facts, that their opinions need to be supported by facts, and that the facts need to be *actual facts*. A structured debate offers students the opportunity to assess resources, take notes, and voice their concerns in a respectful, mature manner.

How-to

Sometimes it is beneficial to have students assigned to the side of the argument they disagree with. In our society we often fail at understanding our opposing viewpoints. Have students research their topic and prepare for the structured debate using notes. In the end, collect notes, a Works Cited, and a reflection on whether researching the opposite side changed their viewpoint at all!

Looking for debate material? Check out . . .

- The New York Times "Our 100 Most Popular Student Questions for Debate and Persuasive Writing"

- The New York Times Room For Debate at www.nytimes.com/roomfordebate

- The IDEA (International Debate Education Association) Database at www.idebate.org

- Intelligence Squared at www.intelligencesquaredus.org

Letters to the Editor (or Somebody Else!)

Description

Middle and high school students often have excellent solutions to large problems, because they thrive on idealism and don't get bogged down in the societal restrictions we often place on ourselves. To show them how to use their voices in ways that are valued and influential, have them write letters instead of essays. They will not only learn all of the same writing and content lessons, but they will produce work that is of higher quality because they know that somebody besides the teacher is reading it and if done well, it may make meaningful change.

How-to

Part of pre-writing for letter research is also identifying the audience and the avenue for getting the letter to the audience. Does it go in an envelope? An email? A newspaper? Is it submitted to a website? Actual publication is part of the research. When they are writing this piece, they also need to pay very serious attention to tone and word choice. Knowing that their words can affect action means recognizing how to write clearly and precisely. When writing a letter, students also need to not just list facts—there needs to be evidence of the author's voice throughout the letter. The facts are simply supporting the writer's intentions. You will be surprised, but many students do not know how to format a letter or address an envelope. Explicit instruction in this often needs to take place, as well.

TED-ish Talks

Description

Who doesn't like a good TED talk? While TED talks run for 17+/− minutes, TED Ed talks run for 6–10 minutes. Seventeen minutes is a long time for a student to prepare a talk and a longer time for a classroom of students to sit and watch several in succession! In these short presentations, students explore a topic they want an audience to think differently about. While I've done these with numerous students, one of my favorites that stands out was by a quiet sophomore girl who got up and explained what social anxiety is, what it looks like, and how we as teachers and students can offer support to those quiet kids we see in school. It was so powerful!

How-to

In this project, students need to think not only about their thesis, but about their call-to-action. What do they want the audience to do? To think differently about? Show students sample TED talks in the field that you are studying and ask them to dissect them as a craft. They should recognize that each talk starts with some kind of opening attention getter. That the speaker seamlessly integrates facts with narrative. That the slides used augment what is being said; they do not reiterate it. (Students are always looking for places with free pictures. My favorites are Unsplash and Morguefile.) I like to show students the short YouTube video, "Five Things Every Presenter Needs to Know About People" by Susan Weinschenk to discuss the confliction behind our audio and video processing channels. When students write their speeches up, they need to write more informally than in an essay or a letter, because it needs to sound conversational. I always ask students to print off their final piece and read it with a pencil in hand so they can hear where transitions and conjunctions need to be added for fluency. The big thing with TED talks is giving students time to practice. Don't just suggest practice—make it part of the project. No unrehearsed talk will ever go well. If so desired, the videos can be recorded and published on your school or library YouTube page for others to view.

Infographics

Description

Infographics are exciting ways to present information. Because 50% of the brain is used to process visual information, we tend to remember more when engaging visual material is given to us (Neomam Studios). Online infographics contain statistics, clipart, arrows, charts, and anything else students want to design. The title can either act as a simplified thesis (Processed Food Can Be Healthy, Too!) or it can be the essential question (Can Processed Food Be Healthy?).

How-to

As students have collected data, they will most likely need to pare down— what is essential to include here? An infographic should not just be a splattering of facts on a page—collectively, they should be proving a point and contributing to the greater message you want your audience to walk away with. They then will need to plan out their infographic. Setting it up and determining what kinds of visuals and charts to use can be tricky at first. Be sure to show them lots of examples of great infographics and direct them to sites that will help them build beautiful visuals.

Some of my favorites are:

- Canva
- Dipity
- Easel.ly
- Piktochart
- Smore
- Venngage

Essays are necessary undertakings that help our students fluently build, develop, and expand on their ideas. Writing with clear focus and purpose, I would argue, is a critical academic skill that needs to be carried into their academic, professional, and personal lives. But in the real world, not every research process ends in a full-blown essay. Our visual media is a thriving world, bursting with sound, color, and image. We live in arenas of stimulating experiences that appeal to our audience on multiple levels. It is as important to introduce our students to methods that allow them to creatively portray their work as it is to introduce them to essay writing.

With Thanks

Recently, I was given a box of letters I wrote to a friend in 7th grade while she spent a year sailing to the Bahamas with a friend. "Have you learned anything about weather, meteorology, or the atmosphere?" I wrote.

> We just got done learning 'bout that, & it is SO FASCINATING! If you haven't, I have to show you my Science Notes, & explain. I mean, it feels so good to have it rain, & understand why. Or, to have a thunderstorm, & understand why it's not so humid after. It was so interesting to learn 'bout!"

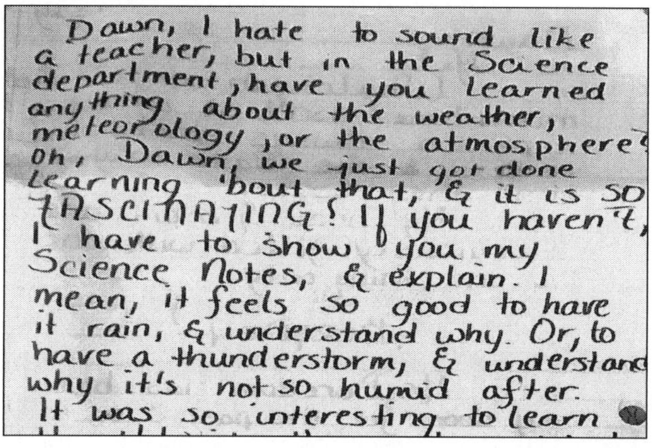

Dawn, I hate to sound like
a teacher, but in the Science
department, have you learned
anything about the weather,
meteorology, or the atmosphere?
Oh, Dawn, we just got done
learning 'bout that, & it is SO
FASCINATING! If you haven't,
I have to show you my
Science Notes, & explain. I
mean, it feels so good to have
it rain, & understand why. Or, to
have a thunderstorm, & understand
why it's not so humid after.
It was so interesting to learn

Figure T.1 My silly 7th grade letter

I use this example not to show how much I loved the colloquial 'bout or that I was a fan of the Oxford comma at age 13, but because while I'd like to think that my interest in research instruction developed out of the classroom and in the library, I might have to admit that I have always been a bit of a research nerd.

It's sometimes difficult to successfully share nerdy passion without sounding pedantic and tedious, and my earliest drafts of this book certainly indicated this phenomenon. What you hold in your hand today, is not just a product of my work, but it is the baby of many people, and for that I owe much gratitude.

I must first thank Kate Messner, who believed in me before I believed I even had an idea, and continued to nudge and push and guide throughout the process. Also, Holly Holland, deserves my thanks for diagnosing my psychoses before I had to confess them, and helping take the intangible and make it practical.

John Norton from MiddleWeb swooped down and breathed life into this project. And Lauren Davis, editor extraordinaire, reminds me routinely of what good writing instruction looks like through her feedback: positivity, suggestions, and recognizing weaknesses as pathways to greatness. She was also patient when I missed a deadline because I was homeless in Costa Rica and then once I did have a home, had no Internet and had to schedule my access around the rainy season's afternoon thunderstorms. Thank you for your support and patience. I am grateful for the autonomy and guidance the teams at Routledge and MiddleWeb have granted me.

Any teacher knows the importance of having a professional tribe. I am surrounded by a multitude of curious, excited, dynamic educators who challenge my thinking and are always willing to suffer through my pontificating over nerdy stuff. And so, I must thank my colleagues at Inter-Lakes High School who incorporate my "what-ifs" into their classrooms. I couldn't think of a more supportive crew to work alongside. I am eternally grateful to Katherine Bassett and my extended professional network through the National Network of State Teachers of the Year (NNSTOY)—they are the people who encourage my best and steer me from my worst. But specifically, this book would not have been finished without the support of Sue who is the other half of my brain; Rachel whose inquisitive mind expanded my horizons; Sarah who gave up many plan periods to talk research; Tom who kept his hand behind my back the entire way; and Chris who helped me develop philosophy while we hiked miles of trails in the White Mountains. And of course, this book certainly would not have taken its shape without Shanna Peeple's friendship and Sunday-afternoon-commiserating conferences. Her critical insight on research and writing processes helped feel not so alone in the writing wilderness.

When alone, in that wilderness, though, my greatest companions have been my dogs. And it seems entirely silly to write a bit of gratitude for two illiterate beings who solely act without reason or logic, let alone research, but any dog owner–writer knows that a warm little snuggle can pull you through the hardest sentences.

I wish I were a neat writer, but my process is messy—physically and mentally—and the people who feel the greatest impact of that are the ones who have to pick up after me—literally and figuratively. My kids, Cecilia, Olivia, and Elliot—all of whom I would like to be when I grow up are my greatest cheerleaders. And my husband, Brandon, who is not only my toughest writing critic, but is the picture of patience and forgiveness, deserves everything from me in payment. Even grocery shopping, cooking dinner, and paying bills on time.

And finally, neither this book nor my career would exist were it not for my students. Their intrepidness in the classroom, their honesty with me, their passion for life, and their desire for justice give me hope that their generation will do good by us. If we work hard to help them develop the skills they need, I assure you we will be in good hands.

Figure T.2 The best dogs a writer can have

#tldnr?

I have amazing family, friends, editors, colleagues, students, and dogs. Without any of them, I would never have finished this book.

Works Consulted

"13 Reasons Why Your Brain Craves Infographics." NeoMam. N.p., n.d. Web.

"Academic Integrity at MIT." What Is Common Knowledge? Academic Integrity at MIT. N.p., n.d. Web.

"Academic Use." Wikipedia. Wikimedia Foundation, n.d. Web.

Barras, Colin. "Can You Learn to Be Creative?" BBC, 14 Mar. 2014. Web.

Bloomberg. Available from www.bloomberg.com/graphics/2015-job-skills-report/ 2015.

"Citing Wikipedia." Wikipedia. Wikimedia Foundation, n.d. Web.

Domonoske, Camila. "Students Have 'Dismaying' Inability To Tell Fake News From Real, Study Finds." The Two-Way. NPR, 23 Nov. 2016. Web.

"English Language Arts Standards." English Language Arts Standards. Common Core State Standards, n.d. Web.

Ghajar, Lee Ann. "Wikipedia: Credible Research Source or Not?" Teaching History.org. National History Clearinghouse, n.d. Web.

Grant, Adam M. *Originals: How Non-conformists Move the World*. N.p.: Viking, 2016. Print.

Harris, Robert A. *The Plagiarism Handbook: Strategies for Preventing, Detecting, and Dealing with Plagiarism*. N.p.: Pyrczak Publ., 2001. Print.

Harris, Robert. "Anti-Plagiarism Strategies for Research Papers." Virtual Salt. N.p., 18 May 2015. Web.

Head, Allison J. "Learning the Ropes: How Freshmen Conduct Course Research Once They Enter College." Rep. The Information School at the University of Washington. N.p.: Project Information Literacy, 2013. Cengage, 5 Dec. 2013. Web.

Heath, Chip, and Dan Heath. "The Curse of Knowledge." *Harvard Business Review*. N.p., Dec. 2006. Web.

Kolowich, Steve. "What Students Don't Know." *Inside Higher Ed*. N.p., 22 Aug. 2011. Web.

Levy, Francesca, and Jonathan Rodkin. "These Are the Job Skills Employers Want but Can't Find." Bloomberg.com. Bloomberg, n.d. Web.

McTighe, Jay, and Grant P. Wiggins. *Essential Questions: Opening Doors to Student Understanding*. N.p.: ASCD, 2013. Print.

Malone-Kircher, Madison. "Your Middle School Teacher Was Wrong About Wikipedia." The Vindicated. NY Mag, 17 Nov. 2016. Web.

McGrew, Sam Wineburg and Sarah. "Why Students Can't Google Their Way to the Truth." *Education Week*. N.p., 1 Nov. 2016. Web.

Meriam, Library. *Evaluating Information – Applying the CRAAP Test*. Chico: University of California, n.d. PDF.

Miller, Peter. "Swarm Theory." Swarm Theory. *National Geographic Magazine*, July 2007.

Mueller, Pam A., and Daniel M. Oppenheimer. "The Pen Is Mightier Than the Keyboard." *Psychological Science* 25.6 (2014): 1159–168. Print.

Pink, Daniel H. *Drive: The Surprising Truth about What Motivates Us*. N.p.: Riverhead, 2012. Print.

Radii. "Brainstorm Effectively: Brainswarming Radii Community." Go Digital. N.p., 30 Sept. 2016. Web.

Ritchhart, Ron. *Making Thinking Visible: How to Promote Engagement, Understanding, and Independence for All Learners*. N.p.: Jossey-Bass, 2011. Print.

Rothstein, Dan. *Make Just One Change: Teach Students to Ask Their Own Questions*. N.p.: Harvard Education, 2011. Print.

Schilling, David Russell. "Knowledge Doubling Every 12 Months, Soon to Be Every 12 Hours." Industry Tap. N.p., 19 Aug. 2013. Web.

Silverman, Craig. "This Analysis Shows How Viral Fake Election News Stories Outperformed Real News on Facebook." BuzzFeed. N.p., 16 Nov. 2016. Web.

Wagner, Tony. *Creating Innovators: The Making of Young People Who Will Change the World*. N.p.: Scribner, 2015. Print.

Wagner, Tony. *Where Our Next Great Innovators Will Come From*. Simon & Schuster Books, 27 Feb. 2012. Available from www.simonandschuster.com/books/Creating-Innovators/Tony-Wagner/9781451611526.

Wiggins, Grant P., and Jay McTighe. *Understanding by Design*. N.p.: Association for Supervision and Curriculum Development, 2008. Print.